HAPPY LIVING

ARVIND UPADHYAY

It is not important how you choose to pronounce or even spell hygge. To paraphrase one of the greatest philosophers of our time—Winnie-the-Pooh—when asked how to spell a certain emotion, "You don't spell it, you feel it." However, spelling and pronouncing hygge is the easy part. Explaining exactly what it is, that's the tricky part. Hygge has been called everything from "the art of creating intimacy," "coziness of the soul," and "the absence of annoyance," to "taking pleasure from the presence of soothing things," "cozy togetherness," and my personal favorite, "cocoa by candlelight". Hygge is about an atmosphere and an experience, rather than about things. It is about being with the people we love. A feeling of home. A feeling that we are safe, that we are shielded from the world and allow ourselves to let our guard down. You may be having an endless conversation about the small or big things in life—or just be comfortable in each other's silent company—or simply just be by yourself enjoying a cup of tea. One December just before Christmas, I was spending the weekend with some friends at an old cabin. The shortest day of the year was brightened by the blanket of snow covering the surrounding landscape. When the sun set, around four in the afternoon, we would not see it again for seventeen hours, and we headed inside to get the fire going. We were all tired after hiking and were half asleep, sitting in a semicircle around the fireplace in the cabin, wearing big sweaters and woolen socks. The only sounds you could hear were the stew boiling, the sparks from the fireplace, and someone having a sip of mulled wine. Then one of my friends broke the silence. "Could this be any more hygge?" he asked rhetorically. "Yes," one of the women said after a moment. "If there was a storm raging outside." We all nodded.

At the Happiness Research Institute, which is an independent think tank focusing on well-being, happiness, and quality of life, we explore the causes and effects of human happiness and work toward improving the quality of life of citizens across the world. Denmark's position as one of the happiest countries in the world has created a lot of media interest. On a weekly basis, I am asked questions like "Why are the Danes so happy?" and "What can we learn from the Danes when it comes to happiness?" from journalists from The New York Times, the BBC, The Guardian, the China Daily, and The Washington Post, among others. In addition, delegations of mayors, researchers, and policy makers from all corners of the earth frequently visit the Happiness Research Institute in pursuit of . . . well . . . happiness—or at least in pursuit of the reasons for the high levels of happiness, well-being, and quality of life people enjoy in Denmark. To many, it is quite the mystery, as besides the horrific weather, Danes are also subject to some of the highest tax rates in the world. Interestingly, there is wide support for the welfare state. The support stems from an awareness of the fact that the welfare model turns our collective wealth into well-being. We are not paying taxes, we are investing in our society. We are purchasing quality of life. The key to understanding the high levels of well-being in Denmark is the welfare model's ability to reduce risk, uncertainty, and anxiety among its citizens and to prevent extreme unhappiness. However, recently, I have also come to realize that there might be an overlooked ingredient in the Danish recipe for happiness—hygge. The word hygge originates from a Norwegian word meaning "well-being". For almost five hundred years, Denmark and Norway were one kingdom, until Denmark lost Norway in 1814. Hygge appeared in written Danish for the first time in the early 1800s, and the link between hygge and well-being or happiness may be no coincidence. Danes are the happiest people in Europe according to the European Social Survey, but they are also the ones who meet most often with their friends and family and feel the calmest and most peaceful. Therefore, it is with good reason that we see a growing interest in hygge. Journalists are touring Denmark searching for hygge; in the UK, a college is now teaching Danish hygge; and around the world, hygge bakeries, shops, and cafés are popping up. But how do you create hygge? How are hygge and happiness linked? And what is hygge exactly? Those are some of the questions this book seeks to answer.

AA few years back, I faced some big questions and daunting struggles. No one would have guessed it: I hid my worries well. But something was off, and I felt alone in my questions. Looking around, it seemed other people had answers I simply couldn't find. Watching them, I wondered what I was missing. I didn't know where to find answers. After all, these aren't questions people bring up in casual conversation. Around me, it seemed, people were doing great—at least that's what they told me. So I smiled harder and pretended it all made sense to me too. I felt more than confused.

I felt alone. When I talked with my doctor about my concerns, he shrugged, "Everyone feels this way." Maybe he thought I'd find this revelation comforting. I didn't. He talked about medications he usually prescribed when people said they felt this way. "Really?" I wondered. "Is that the answer?" Something inside told me there was another way. So I went looking for it. I opened my mind and challenged my assumptions. I read voraciously, took classes, and explored every path I could to learn how others answered life's tough questions about meaning, purpose, and the pursuit of happiness. I looked to philosophy, modern and timeless wisdom, and science. I studied anthropology and religion. I explored real-life stories and tried to increase my self-expression and self-care. Insights came slowly at first. But when I started learning about the brain, something clicked. For the first time, I saw patterns across the different paths to happiness—and even in my own experiences. With increasing clarity, I saw a new light. Neuroscience—the science of the brain—seemed to reveal some of the answers I was seeking. And the more I learned, the clearer those answers became. Today, I still have questions. But they're about what's possible, not about what's holding me back. As I've learned to work with my brain—and studied its role in shaping our life experiences—I'm happier. More energized. More curious, focused, and confident, beyond what I would have imagined a few years back. Nothing could have prepared me for the benefits I've received by learning to understand, and work in accord with, my brain. As I've shared my learning with students and audiences in Silicon Valley and beyond, I see again and again how understanding the brain and working with it—in a word, being mindful—helps us do more of what satisfies us and less of what slows us down. This book offers some of the frameworks that have helped me, and people I've worked with, find more purpose, clarity, and satisfaction. As I talk with people—all kinds of people, from different backgrounds and experiences, whether they've lived with ease or faced real hardship—their questions sound surprisingly like mine did ten years ago. My intention in writing this book is to offer you a shorter path than my process gave me. Navigating unknown terrain was hard, but now that I have a map, I want to share it. Understanding the brain helps give you some control of it, at least some of the time, rather than simply letting it be in charge of you. Brain-aware thinking helps you take charge of an incredibly powerful tool, guiding you to new paths—to focus, a sense of purpose, and even happiness. As you'll learn in the pages ahead, working with your brain gives you new ways to face life with clarity and resilience.

Contents

Foreword

To enjoy good health, to bring true happiness to one's family, to bring peace to all, one must first discipline and control one's own mind. If we can control our mind, we can find the way to Enlightenment, and all wisdom and virtue will naturally come to us.

Happiness is not a station you arrive at, but a manner of traveling. —MARGARET LEE RUNBECK, NOVELIST

Nothing captures the biological argument better than the famous New Age slogan: "Happiness begins within." Money, social status, plastic surgery, beautiful houses, powerful positions—none of these will bring you happiness. Lasting happiness comes only from serotonin, dopamine, and oxytocin. —YUVAL NOAH HARARI, SAPIENS: A BRIEF HISTORY OF HUMANKIND

Take a second. Think whatever you want. It's your brain. Make yourself at home in it. —LIN-MANUEL MIRANDA, PLAYWRIGHT, COMPOSER, ACTOR

1

INSTANT HYGGE: CANDLES

No recipe for hygge is complete without candles. When Danes are asked what they most associate with hygge, an overwhelming 85 percent will mention candles. The word for "spoilsport" in Danish is lyseslukker, which means "the one who puts out the candles", and this is no coincidence. There is no faster way to get to hygge than to light a few candles or, as they are called in Danish, levende lys, or living lights. The American ambassador to Denmark, Rufus Gifford, said of the Danes' love affair with candles: "I mean, it is not just in the living room. It is everywhere. In your classrooms, in your boardrooms. As an American, you think, 'Fire hazard!—how can you possibly have an open flame in your classroom?' It is kind of an emotional happiness, an emotional coziness." The American ambassador is onto something. According to the European Candle Association, Denmark burns more candles per head than anywhere in Europe. Each Dane burns around thirteen pounds of candle wax each year. To put this in context, each Dane consumes around six and a half pounds of bacon per year (yes, bacon consumption per capita is a standard metric in Denmark). The candle consumption is a European record. In fact, Denmark burns almost twice as much candle wax as the runner-up, Austria, with a little under seven pounds per year. However, scented candles are not a big thing. In fact, Asp-Holmblad, Denmark's oldest producer of candles, doesn't even include scented candles in their product range. Scented candles are considered artificial, and Danes prefer natural and organic products. In fact, Danes rank towards the top of the list in Europe when it comes to buying organic. More than half of Danes light candles almost every day during autumn and winter, and only 4 percent say they never light candles, according to a survey by one of the major newspapers in Denmark. During

December, the candle consumption soars to thrice as many, and this is also the time to witness the special candle that is to be burned only in the days leading up to Christmas, namely the kalenderlys—the advent candle. This candle is marked with twentyfour lines, one for each day in December before Christmas, turning it into the slowest countdown clock in the world. Another special candle occasion is May 4, also known as lysfest, or light party. On this evening in 1945, the BBC broadcast that the German forces who had occupied Denmark since 1940 had surrendered. As in many countries during World War II, Denmark was subject to blackouts to prevent enemy aircraft from navigating by city lights. Today, Danes still celebrate the return of the light on this evening by putting candles in their windows. Hyggelige as the Danes may be, there is one serious drawback to being crazy about candles: the soot. Studies show that lighting just one candle fills the air with more microparticles than traffic in a busy street. A study undertaken by the Danish Building Research Institute showed that candles shed more particles indoors than either cigarettes or cooking. Despite Denmark being a highly regulated country, we have yet to see warning labels on candles. Nobody messes with the hygge fanatics. There is now a growing awareness among Danes of the importance of airing out a room after burning candles. Nevertheless, despite the health implications, Danes continue to consume candles in obscene quantities. LAMPS Lighting is not just about candles. Danes are obsessed by lighting in general. I once spent two hours walking around Rome with my girlfriend at the time to find a restaurant that had hyggelig lighting. Danes select lamps carefully and place them strategically to create soothing pools of light. It is an art form, a science, and an industry. Some of the most beautifully designed lamps in the world come from the golden age of Danish design—for example, the lamps of Poul Henningsen, Arne Jacobsen, and Verner Panton. Visit a student on a shoestring budget and you may still encounter a $1,300 Verner Panton lamp in the corner of her hundred-square-foot flat. The rule of thumb is: the lower the temperature of the light, the more hygge. A camera flash is around 5,500 Kelvin (K), fluorescent tubes are 5,000K, incandescent lamps 3,000K, while sunsets and wood and candle flames are about 1,800K. That is your hygge sweet spot. The closest you will ever come to seeing vampires burned by daylight is by inviting a group of Danes for a hygge dinner and then placing them under a 5,000K fluorescent light tube. At first they will squint, trying to examine the torture device you have placed in the ceiling. Then, as dinner begins, observe how they move uncomfortably around in their chairs, compulsively scratching and trying to suppress twitches. The obsession with lighting comes from the lack of contact with it in the natural world from October to March. During this time, *the only resource Denmark has in abundance is darkness. Summers in Denmark are beautiful. When the first rays of light reach the country, Danes awaken from their hibernation and fall over themselves to find spots in the sun. I love summer in Denmark. It is my favorite time of the year. And if it wasn't bad enough that winters are dark and cold and summers are short, Denmark also has 179 days of rain per year. Game of Thrones fans, think of the city of Winterfell. That is why hygge has been refined to the level it has, and why it is seen as part of the national identity and culture in Denmark. Hygge is the antidote to the cold winter, the rainy days, and the duvet of darkness. So while you can have hygge all year round, it is during winter that it becomes not only a necessity but a survival strategy. That is why Danes have a reputation of being hygge fundamentalists and talk about it . . . a lot. My favorite spot in my apartment in Copenhagen is the windowsill in the kitchen-dining area. It is wide enough to sit comfortably in and I've added pillows and blankets to make it a real hyggekrog (see the hygge dictionary in Chapter 2). The radiator underneath the windowsill makes it the perfect place to enjoy a cup of tea on a cold winter night. But what I like about it most is the warm amber glow issuing from every apartment across the courtyard. It's a constantly changing mosaic of radiance as people leave and return home. In part, I owe this view to Poul Henningsen. Inevitably, a well-lit room in Denmark is likely to hold a lamp by the architect and designer all Danes know simply as PH. He was to light fixtures what Edison was to the lightbulb. PH was, like most Danes today, obsessed with light. Some call him the world's first lighting architect, as he devoted his career to exploring the importance of light for our well-being, aiming to develop a lamp that could spread light without subjecting people to a direct glare. Poul Henningsen was born in 1894 and did not grow up with electric light but in the soft glow of petroleum lamps. These were his source of inspiration. His designs shape and refine the power of the electric light yet maintain the softness of the light of a petroleum lamp. It doesn't cost money to light a room correctly—but it does require culture. From the age of eighteen, when I began to experiment with light, I have been searching for harmony in lighting. Human beings are like children. As soon as they get new toys, they throw away their culture and the orgy starts. The electric light gave the possibility of wallowing in light. When, in the evening, from the top of a tram car, you look into all the homes on the first floor, you shudder at how dismal people's homes are. Furniture, style, carpets—everything in the home is unimportant, compared to the positioning of the lighting.*

THE PH LAMP After a decade of experiments with lamps and lighting in his attic, Henningsen presented the first PH lamp in 1925. It gave a softer and *more diffused light by using a series of layered shades to disperse the light yet conceal the lightbulb. In addition, to bring the harsh white light toward the red end of the spectrum, PH gave the inner side of one element of the shade a red colour. His biggest success was PH5, which has metal shades and was launched in 1958, but PH lamps have now been produced in over a thousand different designs. Many of these are not in production anymore, and the rarest lamps can go for more than $25,000 at auction. LE KLINT In 1943, the Klint family started producing lampshades with folding pleats, but in fact they had been designed four decades earlier by Peder Vilhelm Jensen-Klint, a Danish architect, for his own use, as he had designed a petroleum lamp and needed a shade. It became a family business, applying the skills in design, innovation, and business of the sons and daughters of Klint. PANTON VP GLOBE The Panton VP Globe is a pendant lamp that casts calming, diffused light from its center rim. It was designed in 1969 by Verner Panton—the enfant terrible of Danish design who loved to work with modern materials such as plastic and steel. Panton attended the Royal Danish Academy of Fine Arts, Schools of Architecture, Design and Conservation, a leading institution for architecture, which today includes a "light laboratory" that examines daylight and artificial lighting. BETTER THAN PHOTOSHOP Members of one profession might be just as obsessed with lighting as the Danes: photographers. Photography means painting with light, and doing it increases your understanding of light and your ability to see and appreciate it. This might be the reason why I love photography and have taken tens of thousands of pictures over the past ten years, and why my favorite light is the golden hour. The golden hour is roughly the first hour after sunrise and the last hour before sunset. When the sun is low in the sky, the sunlight has to travel through a greater depth of atmosphere. During these times, it produces a warm, soft, diffused light. It is sometimes also called the "magic hour", and I think I have fallen in love with every woman whose picture I have taken at this time of day for that 1/250 of a second. This is the light you want to aim for if you are going for hyggelig lighting indoors. The flattering quality of the lighting will make you and all your friends look "grotto-fabulous." It's better than any Instagram filter. HYGGE TIP: CREATE HYGGELIG LIGHTING You guessed it. Bring out the candles. But remember to air out the room. However, you may also want to consider your electric-light strategy. Usually, several smaller lamps around the room create a more hyggeligt light than one big lamp set in the ceiling. You want to create small caves of light around the room.*

2

IT'S ALL ABOUT THE HYGGE (HAPPY LIVING)

The Danish language has been called many things, but seldom beautiful. Google "Danish sounds like . . . ," and the first two suggestions that appear are "German" and "potato." To foreigners, Danish sounds like someone speaking German with a hot potato in their mouth. To be fair, some people have also suggested it sounds somewhat like a diseased seal choking. Nevertheless, it is rich when it comes to describing hygge. Hygge comes in the form of both a verb and an adjective. Something can be hyggelig(t) (hygge-like): What a hyggelig living room! It was so hyggeligt to see you! Have a hyggelig time! We throw the words hygge and hyggelig around so much that, to foreigners, it might appear excessive. We have to state how hyggelig everything is. All the time. And not just in the hygge moment itself. We talk about how hyggeligt it will be to get together on Friday, and on Monday we will remind each other of how hyggelig Friday was. Hygge is a key performance indicator of most Danish social gatherings. "Honey, do you think our guests hyggede themselves?" (It's the past tense—don't attempt to pronounce it.) Every few weeks, I meet up with a group of guys to play poker. It is quite an international group, with people from Mexico, the United States, Turkey, France, England, India and Denmark. Over the years, we have covered most subjects ranging from women to how to optimize the range of an orange cannon. Due to the diversity of the group, our conversations are always in English. Nevertheless, there is one Danish word that is often used around the table. You guessed it. Often it will come from Danny from Mexico after losing a big hand: "It doesn't matter. I am just here for the hygge." The hygge factor is not just a key performance indicator for social events, it is also a not so unique selling point for cafés and restaurants. Search for "beautiful restaurant" in Danish, and Google will provide you with 7,000 hits. Searching for a "quality restaurant" will give you 9,600 options and "cheap restaurant," 30,600. "Hyggelig restaurant" gives you 88,900 hits on Google. As Lonely Planet points out, "The Danes are obsessed with coziness. All of them. Even the toughest leather-clad biker will recommend a bar based on its 'hygge' factor." It means that everything you learned in that marketing class was wrong. Price, product, place, and promotion can kiss my ass. It is all about the hygge. I live in Copenhagen. Cafés are plentiful, and there is one right across the street from my apartment. Their coffee is an abomination. It tastes like fish (yes, I was surprised too) and costs five euros. I still go there sometimes. They have an open fireplace, so it's hygge. Fireplaces are not unique to Denmark. Neither are candles, cozy company or snuggling up with a cup of tea and a blanket on a stormy night. Danes, however, insist that hygge is uniquely Danish. One third refuse the idea that hygge can be translated into other languages and believe that it is mainly practiced in Denmark. I disagree with that. Danes are not the only ones who can have hygge or identify it, and other languages have similar expressions. The Dutch call it gezelligheid and Germans talk of Gemütlichkeit, a sense of well-being based on good food and good company, and Canadians will recognize it as "hominess." However, while more languages than Danish have similar adjectives for the noun hygge, it seems that only Danes use hygge as a verb, as in "Why don't you come over and hygge with us tonight?" This might be unique. What might also be unique for Denmark when it comes to hygge is how much we talk about it, focus on it, and consider it as a defining feature of our cultural identity and an integral part of the national DNA. In other words, what freedom is to Americans, thoroughness to Germans, and the stiff upper lip to the British, hygge is to Danes. Because of its importance to Danish culture and identity, the Danish language is also rich when it comes to talking about hygge. Danish is an infinite list of compound words. For example, speciallægepraksisplanlægningsstabiliseringsperiode (specialty-doctor-practiceplanning-stabilizing-period) is an actual word. It contains fifty-one letters and could be considered the golden goal of Scrabble. Hygge is no different. You can pretty much add it to any other word in the Danish language. You can be a hyggespreder (someone who spreads the hygge), Friday night is reserved for familiehygge, and socks can be labeled hyggesokker. At the Happiness Research Institute, we have a sign saying: "You are welcome to borrow some woolen hyggesokker if your feet are cold." WHAT'S IN A NAME? Shakespeare famously wrote, in Romeo and Juliet, "What's in a name? That which we call a rose/By any other name would smell as sweet," and I think his point applies to hygge as well. Danes are not the only ones who can enjoy the atmosphere, comfort, and pleasure that comes from being in good company, in front of the fire, with some mulled wine. While an English translation of hygge as coziness may be problematic, because it loses a lot of important associations, we can find a variety of concepts more similar to hygge around the world. GEZELLIGHEID—THE NETHERLANDS Dictionaries tell us that gezelligheid is something cozy, quaint, or nice, but to the Dutch, gezelligheid goes way beyond this. If you want to score some cheap points with the Dutch, go with what President Obama stated when he visited the Netherlands in 2014: "I'm told there's a Dutch word that captures the spirit, which doesn't translate exactly in English, but let me say that my first visit to the Netherlands has been truly gezellig." The Dutch tend to use the word gezellig in a lot of ways—for example, drinking coffee at a gezellig café (read: warm interior, flickering candles, and a sleeping cat). Seeking shelter from the pouring rain at a gezellig bar that serves only vintage beers and plays old records is the purest form of gezelligheid. Sitting in a soulless waiting room for your appointment with the dentist is everything but gezellig, unless a very gezellig friend accompanies you. Are you starting to see the similarities between gezelligheid and hygge? Even though the two are very similar, they are not completely alike, and it's often emphasized that gezelligheid is a bit more social than hygge. To test whether this is the case, we carried out a small survey among Dutch people, and the results seem to back up this theory. On most of the indicators, it seems that Danes experience hygge the same way the Dutch experience gezelligheid. The concept is important in both cultures, and candles, fireplaces, and Christmas are core elements in hygge and gezelligheid. However, the notion that gezelligheid has a more outgoing dimension than hygge is also supported by the data we collected. The majority of Dutch people (57 percent) agree that you experience the most gezelligheid outside of your home, while only 27 percent of Danes find that it's most hyggeligt to go out. In addition, 62 percent of the Dutch agree that summer is the most gezellig season of the year, while Danes prefer autumn in terms of hygge. KOSELIG—NORWAY For Norwegians, everything should, ideally, be koselig. Yet again, do not mistake this word for "coziness" (say the Norwegians). More than anything, koselig is a feeling of warmth, intimacy, and getting together. A perfect koselig evening would consist of good food on the table, warm colors around you, a group of good friends, and a fireplace, or at least some lighted candles. HOMINESS—CANADA Canadians use the word hominess to describe a state of shutting out the outside world. It implies a feeling of community, warmth, and togetherness, but hominess also refers to things that resemble home or echo the feeling of home. Thus it has both a physical and a symbolic dimension: it describes how property can be homey if *it's authentic and "real" and how a situation can be homey if it somehow brings to mind the state or feeling of seeking shelter and shutting out the outside world. So, just like hygge, hominess very much implies a feeling of authenticity, warmth, and togetherness. GEMÜTLICHKEIT—GERMANY Germans use the word Gemütlichkeit to cover the state of warmth, friendliness, and belonging, and often to describe the atmosphere at a German beer garden. Visiting an Oktoberfest in Germany, you are even likely to hear the song "Ein Prost der Gemütlichkeit" ("A Toast to Coziness"). HYGGE IS FOR EVERYONE The list of concepts above doesn't only provide evidence that it is possible for people other than Danes to experience hygge but also that they already do. While the concepts across countries aren't completely identical, what they all share is that they are more developed and complex versions of a feeling of coziness, warmth, and togetherness. The various words denote groups of different activities and settings that generate similar and related feelings, which have merged into linguistic concepts. Danish hygge and Dutch gezelligheid may stand out a bit from the others, though, as they are so integrated in daily conversation and lifestyle. But one could ask whether this is in any way beneficial. It may be difficult to provide a simple answer to this question. But it is worth mentioning that, according to the European Social Survey, Denmark and the Netherlands are among the countries with the fewest people who seldom enjoy life or rarely feel calm and relaxed. Also, these two countries represent the very top of the official happiness charts commissioned by the UN. So what's in a name? On the one hand, the specific name has no value in itself. Hygge works just as well as hominess or gezelligheid. On the other hand, we use names to capture that feeling of coziness, warmth, and togetherness, to shape it into a more fixed concept, and eventually, we develop a phenomenon that marks our unique cultural traits. Throughout this book, I will point toward things, experiences, and moments that are hygge so you will come to an understanding of exactly what hygge is. HYGGE DICTIONARY Our words shape our actions. So here are some new words that will help you get your hygge on. Fredagshygge/ Søndagshygge [Fredashooga/Sundashooga] Hygge you have on Fridays or Sundays. After a long week, fredagshygge usually means the family curling up on the couch together watching TV. Søndagshygge is about having a slow day with tea, books, music, blankets, and perhaps the occasional walk if things go crazy. "A fredagshygge tradition in the family was candy and watching a Disney movie." Hyggebukser [hoogabucksr] That one pair of pants you would never wear in public but are so comfortable that they are likely to be, secretly, your favorites. "She just needed a day for herself, so she stayed at home in her hyggebukser, wore no makeup, and just watched television all day." Hyggehjørnet [hoogajornet] To be in the mood for hygge. Literal meaning: "the corner of hygge." "I am in hyggehjørnet." Hyggekrog [hoogacrow] The nook of a kitchen or living room where one can sit and have a hyggelig time. "Let's sit in the hyggekrog." Hyggeonkel [hoogaunkel] A person who plays with the kids and may be a little too lenient. Literal meaning: "the uncle of hygge." "He is such a hyggeonkel." Hyggesnak [hoogasnak] Chitchat or cozy conversation that doesn't touch on controversial issues. "We hyggesnakkede for a couple of hours." Hyggestund [hoogastun] A moment of hygge. "He poured himself a cup of coffee and sat in his window for a hyggestund." Uhyggeligt [uh-hoogalit] While hygge and hyggelig may be difficult to translate into English, it is not the case when it comes to the antonym of hygge. Uhyggeligt (un-hygge) means "creepy" or "scary," and this provides us with some insight into how central the feeling of safety is to hygge. "Walking alone through the woods at night is uhyggeligt if you hear a wolf howling." As my friend pointed out in the cabin in Sweden, the evening would have been even more hygge if there had been a storm outside. Perhaps hygge is even more hygge if there is a controlled element of danger—of uhygge. A storm, thunder, or a scary movie.*

WHERE DOES HYGGE COME FROM? *Hygge appeared in written Danish for the first time in the early 1800s, but the word is actually Norwegian in origin. Between 1397 and 1814, Denmark and Norway were one kingdom. Danes and Norwegians still understand each other's languages today. The original word in Norwegian means well-being. However, hygge might originate from the word hug. Hug comes from the 1560s word hugge, which means "to embrace." The word hugge is of unknown origin—maybe it originates from the Old Norse hygga, which means "to comfort," which comes from the word hugr, meaning "mood." In turn, that word comes from the Germanic word hugjan, which relates to the Old English hycgan, meaning "to think, consider." Interestingly, consideration, mood, comfort, hug and well-being may all be words to describe elements of what hygge is today. HYGGE TIP: GET YOUR DANISH ON Start throwing those hygge words around. Invite your friends for a hyggelig evening and create compound words like there is no tomorrow. You may also want to put the hygge manifesto on your fridge to remind*

you to hygge every day. A GLOBAL CONVERSATION ABOUT HYGGE Hygge seems to be the talk of the town these days. "Hygge: A heart-warming lesson from Denmark" writes the BBC; "Get cozy: why we should all embrace the Danish art of 'hygge.'" says The Telegraph; and Morley College in London is now teaching students how to hygge. The Hygge Bakery in Los Angeles is providing Danish romkugler [rum-cool-r] (rum balls), rum-flavored chocolate treats, originally made by Danish bakers to use up leftover pastry. In the book The Danish Way of Parenting, you can find extensive chapters on how hygge is the way to raise the happiest children in the world. THE HYGGE MANIFESTO 1. ATMOSPHERE Turn down the lights. 2. PRESENCE Be here now. Turn off the phones. 3. PLEASURE Coffee, chocolate, cookies, cakes, candy. Gimme! Gimme! Gimme! 4. EQUALITY 4. EQUALITY "We" over "me." Share the tasks and the airtime. 5. GRATITUDE Take it in. This might be as good as it gets. 6. HARMONY It's not a competition. We already like you. There is no need to brag about your achievements. 7. COMFORT Get comfy. Take a break. It's all about relaxation. 8. TRUCE No drama. Let's discuss politics another day. 9. TOGETHERNESS Build relationships and narratives. "Do you remember the time we . . . ?" 10. SHELTER This is your tribe. This is a place of peace and security.

3

TOGETHERNESS

——❦——

LIKE A HUG WITHOUT TOUCHING Every year, my friends and I go skiing in the Alps (the last time, someone even packed candles). We all enjoy the speed, the thrill, the flow, and the exercise of the slopes, but to me, the best part of the day is the hour after we come back to our cabin. Your feet ache, your body is used and tired, you find a chair on the balcony, and the distinct sound of Grand Marnier being poured tells you that coffee is ready. More people come to the balcony, you are all still wearing your ski clothes, too tired to change, too tired to talk, too tired for anything but to enjoy one another's silent company, take in the view, and breathe in the air of the mountain. When I give lectures about happiness research, I ask the audience to close their eyes and tell them to think of the last time they felt really happy. Sometimes people become a little uneasy, but I assure them that I am not going to ask them to share their memory with the rest of the class. You can almost pinpoint the moment when people have their happy memory in their mind, as peaceful smiles light up the room. When I ask people to raise their hand if they were with others in their memories, usually nine out of ten do so. Of course, this is not a scientific method and therefore proves nothing, but it does allow people to attach a memory and an emotion to the dry statistics I then launch at them. The reason why I want them to remember this is that, in all the work I have done within the field of happiness research, this is the point I am surest about: the best predictor of whether we are happy or not is our social relationships. It is the clearest and most recurrent pattern I see when I look at the evidence on why some people are happier than others. The question is then how to shape our societies and our lives to allow our social relationships to flourish. One answer is, of course, to focus on a healthy work– life balance. And many look at Denmark with envy when it comes to this. "We were not surprised to read last week that the Danes topped the UN's first World Happiness Report,"

Cathy Strongman wrote in The Guardian. She had moved from Finsbury Park in London to Copenhagen three years earlier, with her husband and their daughter. Our quality of life has skyrocketed and our once staunch London loyalism has been replaced by an almost embarrassing enthusiasm for everything "Dansk." The greatest change has been the shift in work–life balance. Whereas previously we might snatch dinner once Duncan escaped from work at around nine, he now leaves his desk at five. Work later than 5.30, and the office is a morgue. Work at the weekend, and the Danes think you are mad. The idea is that families have time to play and eat together at the end of the day, every day. And it works. Duncan bathes and puts our 14-month-old daughter Liv to bed most nights. They are best buddies, as opposed to strangers who try to reacquaint at the weekend. Cathy Strongman, The Guardian Some have described the Danish workplace as something like the opening credits of The Flintstones. Come five o'clock, everyone has left before you can say "Yabba dabba doo!" People with children usually leave at four; those without, at five. Everybody leaves, heading home to cook dinner. As a manager, I avoid scheduling meetings that would end after four if I have parents on my team, so they can pick up their kids at the usual time. On average, 60 percent of Europeans socialize with friends, family, or colleagues a minimum of once a week. The corresponding average in Denmark is 78 percent. While you can hygge by yourself, hygge mostly happens in small groups of close friends or family. Hygge is also a situation where there is a lot of relaxed thoughtfulness. Nobody takes center stage or dominates the conversation for long stretches of time. Equality is an important element in hygge—a trait that is deeply rooted in the Danish culture—and also manifests itself in the fact that everybody takes part in the chores of the hyggelig evening. It is more hyggeligt if we all help to prepare food, instead of having the host alone in the kitchen. Time spent with others creates an atmosphere that is warm, relaxed, friendly, down-to-earth, close, comfortable, snug, and welcoming. In many ways, it is like a good hug, but without the physical contact. It is in this situation that you can be completely relaxed and yourself. The art of hygge is therefore also the art of expanding your comfort zone to include other people. WHAT'S LOVE GOT TO DO WITH IT? OXYTOCIN Someone puts a hand on your shoulder, gives you a kiss, or caresses your cheek and you instantly feel calm and happy. Our bodies work like that: it is a wonderful thing. Touch releases the hormone oxytocin, which makes us feel happy and reduces stress, fear, and pain. But when do we experience the pleasure of having oxytocin flowing through our body? A widespread saying is that hugs make us happier, and that is true— oxytocin starts flowing in intimate situations, and helps us connect to each other. Therefore, it is also called "the *cuddle hormone" or the "love hormone." Hygge is an intimate activity often connected with coziness and some company, which leads one to the conclusion that the body will make oxytocin flow during these events. Cuddling pets has the same effect as cuddling another person—we feel loved, warm, and safe, which are three key words in the concept of hygge. Oxytocin is released when we're physically close to another person's body, and can be described as a "social glue," since it keeps society together by means of cooperation, trust, and love. Maybe that is why Danes trust complete strangers to such a great extent; they hygge a lot, and hyggelige activities release oxytocin, which decreases hostility and increases social connection. Also, warmth and fullness release this hormone. Good food, candles, fireplaces, and blankets are constant companions to hygge. In a way, hygge is all about oxytocin. Could it be that simple? Perhaps it is not a coincidence that everything that has to do with hygge makes us feel happy, calm, and safe. HAPPY TOGETHER Being with other people is a key part of hygge, but as a happiness researcher, I can also testify that it might be the most important ingredient to happiness. There is broad agreement among happiness researchers and scientists that social relations are essential for people's happiness. According to the World Happiness Report commissioned by the United Nations, "While basic living standards are essential for happiness, after the baseline has been met, happiness varies more with quality of human relationships than income." The importance of our relationships has even led to attempts to evaluate them in monetary terms. "Putting a Price Tag on Friends, Relatives, and Neighbors: Using Surveys of Life Satisfaction to Value Social Relationships," a study undertaken in the United Kingdom in 2008, estimated that an increase in social involvements may produce an increase of life satisfaction equivalent to an extra $110,000 a year. I see this link between our relationships and our happiness again and again, in global data and surveys, as well as Danish ones. One example is a city study we conducted a few years ago at the Happiness Research Institute, in the town of Dragør, just outside Copenhagen. We were working with the city council to measure happiness and life satisfaction among the citizens. Together, we developed recommendations on how to improve quality of life in the city. As part of the exploration, we surveyed both how satisfied people were with their social relationships and how happy they were overall. Here we found—as we always do—a very strong correlation. The more satisfied people are with their social relationships, the happier they are in general. As I mentioned before, the relationship factor is usually the best predictor of whether people are happy or not. If I cannot ask people directly how happy they are, I ask them how satisfied they are with their social relationships, because that gives me the answer. An overall* *satisfaction with our relationships is one thing; the everyday joy of good company yet another. And here, Nobel Prize-winning psychologist Daniel Kahneman's Day Reconstruction Method may shed some light on the effect of hygge. The method prompts people to go through a normal day, rating how pleased or annoyed or depressed they feel during a range of activities. In what has become a classic study from 2004, a group of scientists at Princeton, led by Dr. Kahneman, had 909 women in Texas participate in an experiment. The women would fill out a long diary and questionnaire detailing everything they had done the day before and rating it on a seven-point scale: what did they do and at what time, who were they with, and how did they feel during each activity? Perhaps unsurprisingly, the group of researchers found that commuting to work, doing housework, and facing a boss were among the least pleasant activities, while sex, socializing, eating and relaxing were the most enjoyable. Of course, socializing, eating, and relaxing are also main ingredients of hygge. According to the "belongingness hypothesis", we have a basic need to feel connected with others, and close, caring bonds with other people play a major part in our motivation and behavior. Among the evidence for the belongingness hypothesis is the fact that people across the world are born with the ability and motivation to form close relationships, that people are reluctant to break bonds once they have been formed, and that married or cohabiting people live longer than single people (although this last is in part due to an enhanced immune system). "Our relationships affect our happiness! Well, gosh, thank you, happiness research!" Yes, as scientists, we can find it quite frustrating to spend years looking into the question of why some people are happier than others and then find an answer that we all knew anyway. Nevertheless, now we have the numbers, the data, and the evidence to support the notion, and we can and should make use of them when we shape our policies, our societies, and our lives. We are social creatures, and the importance of this is clearly seen when one compares the satisfaction people feel in relationships with their overall satisfaction with life. The most important social relationships are close relationships in which you experience things together with others, and experience being understood; where you share thoughts and feelings, and both give and receive support. In one word: hygge. That may be why Danes prefer smaller circles of friends when they are looking for hygge. Of course, you can have a hyggelig time if there are more people, but Danes would rather a smaller group of people for a hyggelig time. Almost 60 percent of Danes say the best number of people for hygge is three to four. THE DARK SIDE OF HYGGE Hanging out with your close friends in a tightly knit social network, where you all go way back together and know each other well, definitely has its benefits. But in recent years I have also come to realize that there is a severe drawback to a social landscape like this: it doesn't readily admit newcomers. Every person I've met who has moved to Denmark tells me the same thing. It is close to impossible to penetrate the social circles there. Or at least it requires years and years of hard work and persistence. Admittedly, Danes are not good at inviting new people into their friendship circles. In part, this is due to the concept of hygge; it would be considered less hyggeligt if there were too many new people at an event. So getting into a social circle requires a lot of effort and a lot of loneliness on the way. The good thing is, in the words of my friend Jon, "Once you are in, you are in." Once you have broken through, you can trust you will have formed lifelong friendships. HYGGE—SOCIALIZING FOR INTROVERTS While I was researching this book, I gave a lecture to a group of American students who were spending a term in Copenhagen. I often use lectures as opportunities to gather input and inspiration for what I am currently researching, and this was no different, so I steered the discussion on toward relationship between well-being and hygge. One student who had been quiet in the previous discussions raised her hand. "I am an introvert," she said. "And, to me, hygge is such a wonderful thing." Her point was that in the United States, she was used to taking part in social activities with a lot of people, a lot of fast networking, and much excitement. In short, she was in the realm of the extroverts. In Denmark, she found that the way social activities are organized suited her much more—and that hygge was the best thing that could happen for introverts. It was a way of being social without being draining for them. I thought that this was perhaps the most insightful thing I had heard in a long time and promised her I would steal her insight and put it in this book. It is known that introverts derive their energy from within, while extroverts derive theirs from external stimulation. Introverts are often seen as loners, while extroverts are the ones to surround yourself with if you want to have a good time. Introversion is often wrongly linked with shyness, and although social events are not for everyone and might leave an introvert overstimulated and exhausted, social introverts do exist (just as calm extroverts do). This may sound a bit clichéd, but introverts often prefer to devote their "social time" to loved ones whom they know very well, to have meaningful conversations or to sit down and read a book with something warm to drink. This happens to have a very high hygge factor—great, right? Introverts are social, but in a different way. There is not one single way of being social, but it might feel like there are right and wrong ways. Just because introverts are drained by too many external stimuli doesn't mean they don't want to hang out with other people. Hygge is a way of socializing that can suit introverts: they can have a relaxing and cozy night with a couple of friends without having to include a lot of people and a lot of activity. Introverts might want to stay at home instead of attending a big party with a lot of people they don't know, and hygge becomes an option, something in between socializing and relaxing. It makes these two worlds go hand in hand, which is great news for both introverts and extroverts, since it becomes something of a compromise. So, to all you introverts out there, do not feel embarrassed or boring for being a person who prefers things that are hygge. And to all extroverts: light some candles, put on some soothing music, and embrace your inner introvert, just for the night. HYGGE TIP: HOW TO MAKE MEMORIES It is common knowledge that the best part of memories is making them. Start a new tradition with your friends or family. It might be playing board games on the first Friday of every month, or celebrating the summer solstice by the water. In fact it can be whatever meaningful activity will knit the group more tightly together over the years.*

4

FOOD AND DRINK

YOU ARE WHAT YOU EAT *If hygge was a person, I think it would be Alice Waters. With a casual, rustic, and slow approach to life, she embodies many of the key elements of hygge—and she also seems to understand the value of good, hearty food in the company of good people. New Nordic food has gotten a lot of attention in the last few years. The center of attention has been Noma, which opened in 2003 and has been rated the best restaurant in the world four times since 2010. While a dish consisting of live shrimp covered in ants may make the headlines, it is relatively far from everyday Danish cuisine. Traditional Danish lunch includes a budget version of smørrebrød (open-faced sandwiches) on rye bread with pickled herring or leverpostej (liver paste—a spreadable mixture of baked, chopped pig's liver and lard). I bet you think those ants are beginning to look appetizing. For dinner, 50 Shades of Meat and Potatoes would be an apt title for a traditional Danish cookbook. Danes are meat lovers, and on average, every person consumes around 105 pounds of meat per year—with pork being the nation's favorite. The high level of meat, confectionery and coffee consumption in Denmark is directly linked to hygge. Hygge is about being kind to yourself—giving yourself a treat, and giving yourself, and each other, a break from the demands of healthy living. Sweets are hyggelige. Cake is hyggeligt. Coffee or hot chocolate are hyggeligt, too. Carrot sticks, not so much. Something sinful is an integral component of the hygge ritual. But it should not be something fancy or extravagant. Foie gras is not hyggeligt. But a hearty stew is. Popcorn is. Especially if we all share the same bowl. LET'S SIN TOGETHER A couple of years ago, I visited a friend of mine and his family. His daughter was four at the time, and over dinner she turned to me and asked, "What is your job?" "I try to find what makes people happy," I replied. "That's easy." She shrugged. "Sweets." When it comes to happiness, I am not sure the answer is that simple, but she might have been onto something when it comes to hygge. Danes are crazy about confectionery, and a majority of people associate it with hygge: gummy bears, licorice and flødeboller [fleu-the-ball-r], chocolate domes stuffed with cream. In fact, according to a report by Sugar Confectionery Europe, the annual consumption of confectionery in Denmark is 18 pounds per person, making Danes second only to the Finns as the people who eat more sweets than anyone in the world, twice the European average. Also, by 2018, Denmark is expected to overtake Finland as the world's most sweet-crazed country. And it is not just sweets Danes are crazy about. Cake, anyone? CAKE Cake is most definitely hyggeligt, and we Danes eat a lot of it. Cake is a common sight in our offices. Jon is one of my poker buddies, and he and I meet over a pint at his favorite bar in Copenhagen, Lord Nelson, to discuss hygge and our Danish cake obsession. "We do walks by the meeting rooms to scout and monitor leftover cake. We call it cake watch," he told me. "And this is just for internal meetings. If clients are coming, then there will be petits fours on top." Jon is right. Cakes and pastries make everything hyggeligt, both eating them and baking them. They also bring an atmosphere of casualness to any business meeting. However, most cakes are eaten outside the office, at home or in cake shops. One of the most popular and traditional ones is La Glace, Denmark's oldest confectionery shop, established in 1870. Their selection of cakes, including cakes named after famous Danes like Hans Christian Andersen and Karen Blixen, looks like something out of a dream. Their most famous cake is perhaps "sport cake," which is essentially an ocean of whipped cream and so not exactly the breakfast of sports champions. The name derives from the fact that the cake was first produced for the premiere of a play called Sports Man in 1891. The old ideals, the interior, the cakes and pastries and the beautiful rooms in which one sits down to enjoy a sweet masterpiece scream hygge all over Copenhagen. KAGEMAND They say that your superheroes say a lot about you. Americans have Superman, Spiderman, and Batman. Danes have . . . well . . . Cakeman. Okay, so he is not a superhero per se, but he is as popular as his American colleagues at birthday parties. Cakeman (Kagemand [Cai-man]) is a traditional element at Danish birthday parties for children. It looks like a large-scale gingerbread man, is made of a sweet dough with lots of sugar and butter, and is decorated with sweets, Danish flags, and candles. If only we could add bacon to the recipe, we would have all things essentially Danish in one place. Part of the tradition is that the birthday boy or girl cuts the throat of the Cakeman while the other kids scream. "Happy birthday, darling. Now cut the throat of Cakeman." How is that for a hyggelig Nordic-noir birthday? PASTRIES A pastry that is typically Danish is . . . well . . . a Danish. It is not every nationality* *that gets a butter-infused dough with gooey cream in the middle named after it. Usually, it is the kind of nation that has lost every war they have participated in for centuries. However, in Denmark, Danish pastries are called wienerbrød (Vienna bread), as Danish pastry recipes were first developed by chefs who had been to Vienna in the middle of the nineteenth century. Some of the pastries have charming names such as "snails" or "the baker's bad eye," but names aside, they are delicious and good for hygge. Also, if you are looking to spread joy and cheer in a Danish office, just shout out the word "Bon-kringle!" Kringle is a classic Danish pastry and bon means receipt. The concept behind bon-kringle is that when you buy cake and pastry worth 1,000 kroner (around $140) at your local bakery, if you present the receipts, the baker will give you a free kringle. It's like a pastry loyalty card—but without the loyalty card. DIY Getting your hands dirty by baking at home is a hyggelig activity that you can do by yourself or with friends and family. Few things contribute more to the hygge factor than the smell of freshly baked goods. The result does not need to look like something out of a Disney movie—in fact, the more rustic, the more hygge it is. For some time now, sourdough has been a hit among a lot of Danes. The slowness of the process and the feeling of taking care of a living thing makes it all the more hyggeligt. Some Danes talk about their dough as if it were their baby, which they feed and care for. Sourdough is basically a gastronomic alternative to The Sims. HOT DRINKS My team of researchers ran a survey among Danes to find out what people associate hygge with. I had put my money on candles, but I was wrong. Candles came second, while hot drinks took first place. Hot drinks are what 86 percent of Danes associate with hygge. It might be tea, hot chocolate, or mulled wine, but the Danes' favorite hot drink is coffee. If you love Danish TV dramas like Borgen or The Killing, you will be familiar with the Danes' love of coffee. Hardly a scene goes by without someone ordering a coffee, brewing coffee, or one person looking at another while asking, "Coffee?" Danes are the world's fourth biggest coffee drinkers and consume around 33 percent more per capita than Americans. "Live life today like there is no coffee tomorrow." The link between coffee and hygge is evident in the Danish language. Kaffehygge, another compound word, this one consisting of coffee and hygge, is everywhere. "Come to kaffehygge," kaffehygge and cake, workout and kaffehygge, yarn and kaffehygge. Kaffehygge is everywhere. There is even a website dedicated to kaffehygge that states, "Live life today like there is no coffee tomorrow." So while you can hygge without coffee, having some definitely helps. There is something comforting about having a warm cup of coffee in your hands. It is definitely conducive to hygge. ADDICTED TO HYGGE? You can't buy happiness, but you can buy cake, and that* *is almost the same thing—at least, that might be our brain's opinion. Imagine opening the door to a coffee shop. Tempting aromas from all the sweet things on the counter hit you as you step inside, and when you see all the pastries and cakes you feel happy. You choose your favorite cake, and when you take the first bite, a feeling of euphoria spreads through your body. Oh yes, that is good. But have you thought about why you feel so happy when eating sugary food? In the basal forebrain there is something called the nucleus accumbens. It is a part of the brain's reward system and has a significant role when it comes to motivation, pleasure, and reinforcement. Like all other vertebrates, we have this system because it is important that we feel pleasure when doing things like eating food and having sex, since these things are vital for our species' survival. When you are doing something that is considered rewarding, a chemical substance is released in the brain, and the signal substance dopamine is activated. Close to the nucleus accumbens, there is an area called the ventral tegmental area, and dopamine is released from there in reward situations. It is when dopamine is transferred from nerve fibers to receptors in different parts of the brain that we experience pleasure. Memories of a pleasurable event are stored in the cerebral cortex so we won't forget them. It may sound strange, but in a way, you could say the brain creates addictions for our survival. When we are born, the first thing we taste is sweet breast milk. Liking sweet food is beneficial for our survival, and that is why we experience feelings of joy when eating cakes and other sugary things, and why we find it hard to stop. Our body has taught us to continue doing things that are rewarded. It's the same thing that calls when it comes to fat and salt. In short, we associate a certain kind of food with the feeling of pleasure, which makes us want more. Hygge is something that is supposed to be and feel good for you, and that means if you want to eat cake, have some cake. But at the same time, we must know when to stop. It is not very hyggeligt to have a stomachache. SLOW FOOD'S CHUBBY COUSIN So confectionery, cakes, and pastries are hyggelige. But there is more to hygge food than increasing your body mass. Hygge may be comfort food. But hygge food is also very much slow food. How hyggelig a food is also lies in its preparation. The rule of thumb is: the longer a dish takes to cook, the more hyggelig it is. Preparing hygge food is about enjoying the slow process of it, about appreciating the time you spend and the joy of preparing something of value. It is about your relationship with the meal. That is why homemade jams are more hyggelige than bought ones. Every bite will take you back to that summer day when you picked the fruit and the entire house smelled of strawberries. Especially in the wintertime, I enjoy spending the best part of a weekend afternoon cooking something that requires hours baking in the oven or simmering on the stove. The process can even be extended by visiting a great farmers' market, carefully selecting the vegetables in season or having a chat with the butcher about which meat he would recommend for a slow-cooked stew. Having a pot simmering on the stove while you are reading a book in your hyggekrog is not only the sound of hygge but the essence of hygge. The only reason to get up is to add a bit more red wine to the stew. It is important to stress that the process need not revolve around the simmering of some meaty old Nordic cuisine. It is about the process, not the end product. Last summer, I tried to make limoncello. Part of the process is that you leave the peel of several lemons soaking in alcohol for over a week, for the alcohol to absorb the flavor and the color of the peel. Every day after work I would come home, open the fridge, and take a good sniff to see how my concoction was progressing. The end result was so-so, but the enjoyment from monitoring the progress of the bottle in the fridge was hygge all the way. HYGGE RECIPES Five recipes that will definitely get the hygge going. SKIBBERLABSKOVS BRAISED PORK CHEEKS IN DARK BEER WITH POTATOCELERIAC MASH BOLLER I KARRY GLØGG SNOBRØD SNOBRØD SKIBBERLABSKOVS (SKIP-ER-LAP-SCOWS) SKIPPER STEW This dish is a hearty down-to-earth stew, originally made on ships (hence the name), and is great for a brisk autumn day. Instead of brisket, you can use leftover meat, making it even more down-to-earth and hyggelig. Serves 4–6. Cooking time 1 hour and 15 minutes. 1½ pounds brisket 3 onions 7 tablespoons butter 3–4 bay leaves 10–12 black peppercorns 4 cups chicken stock 3½ pounds potatoes Salt and pepper A handful of chives 4–6 pickled beets Rye bread 1. Cut the brisket into bite-size cubes. 2. Peel and chop the onions. 3. Melt the butter in a thick-bottomed pot or Dutch oven and sauté the onions until they are translucent (they should not brown). 4. Add the meat, bay leaves, and peppercorns, then pour the boiling chicken stock into the pot. It should just cover the meat and onions. 5. Cover and leave to simmer for about forty-five minutes. Peel the potatoes and cut them into bite-size pieces. 6. Put half of the potatoes on top of the meat and put the lid back on. 7. After fifteen minutes, stir the contents of the pot and add the rest of the potatoes—and a bit of extra chicken stock if needed. Simmer for another fifteen to twenty minutes on low heat, remembering to stir frequently so the stew doesn't burn on the bottom. The aim is for the meat to be sitting in a potato mash but for there still to be whole pieces of tender potato. 8. Season with salt and pepper, and serve hot with a pat of butter, a generous amount of chives, one pickled beet per person, and rye bread. BRAISED PORK CHEEKS IN DARK BEER WITH POTATO-CELERIAC MASH This is one of my favorite winter dishes. It needs to simmer for a long time on the stove to increase the hygge factor, and* *to allow you to spend time with a glass of wine and your favorite book in the meantime. Serves 4. Cooking time 1 hour and 45 minutes–2 hours. For the braised pork cheeks: 10–12 pork cheeks Salt and pepper 1 tablespoon butter ⅛ celeriac, peeled and roughly chopped 1 carrot, peeled and roughly chopped 1 onion, peeled and roughly chopped 1 tomato, quartered 1 pint of dark beer or ale For the potato-celeriac mash: 1¾ pounds potatoes ¼ celeriac, peeled scant 1 cup milk 2 tablespoons butter Handful chopped parsley and bread for serving Braised pork cheeks: 1. Dry the pork cheeks with a paper towel and season with the salt and pepper. 2. Let the butter turn golden in a saucepan over medium to high heat. Add the meat and brown it on all sides, roughly three to four minutes in total. 3. Add the celeriac, carrot, and onion and let them brown before adding the tomato. 4. Pour in the beer. Add water if necessary to cover the meat and vegetables. 5. Turn the heat down low and simmer for about an hour and a half, until the meat is tender. 6. Remove the meat but continue boiling to reduce the sauce, then put it through a sieve and season. Potato-celeriac mash: 1. Cut the potatoes and celeriac into bite-size pieces. 2. Boil the potatoes and celeriac until tender, then drain and mash the vegetables. 3. Warm the milk in the pan, and add it and the butter to the mash. Season. 4. Serve the braised pork cheeks on a bed of mash. You may add a sprinkle of parsley and some bread* to mop up the sauce. GLØGG (GLOEG) MULLED WINE No December is complete without the traditional gløgg. Danes will meet at bars or invite friends and family over to wish each other a Merry Christmas over this warm, spicy wine. Serves 6–10. Cooking time 20 minutes (plus soaking time for raisins) For the gløgg essence: 4 handfuls of raisins 10 ounces port 1 bottle of heavy red wine, such as Beaujolais or Côtes du Rhone* 1 cup brown sugar (preferably a brown sugar that consists of sugar crystals and cane syrup—but normal brown sugar will do) 20g cinnamon sticks (8 to 10 sticks) 20g allspice (whole) 20g cloves (whole) 10g cardamom (whole) For the gløgg: 2 bottles of heavy red wine, such as Beaujolais or Côtes du Rhone ¾ cup brown rum ¾ cup akvavit (or vodka) Peel of 1 orange ¾ cup freshly squeezed orange juice 1 cup chopped almonds 1. Soak the raisins in the port, preferably for 24 hours. 2. Start by making the gløgg essence. Pour the bottle of red wine into a pot, add the sugar and cinnamon, allspice, cloves, and cardamom, and heat to just below boiling point. Turn off the heat and allow to cool, then strain out the aromatics. 3. Add the additional bottles of red wine, spirits, orange peel and juice to the gløgg essence. Again, heat to just below boiling point, and then add the raisins, port and the almonds. Serve warm. SNOBRØD (SNO-BROEÐ)* TWISTBREAD This dish is not likely to be featured at Noma any time soon. It is not the fanciest bread you'll ever have, but the process of making it gets top marks for hygge and kids* *love it. Makes 6 pieces. Cooking time 1 hour and 15 minutes (including 1 hour for the dough to rest). 2 tablespoons butter 1 cup milk 6½ teaspoons yeast 2 teaspoons sugar ¾ teaspoon salt 3⅛ cup flour 1. Melt the butter in a saucepan and add the milk. Heat until lukewarm. Add the yeast and dissolve. 2. Pour the mix into a large bowl and add the other ingredients to make a dough, but save a little bit of the flour. Knead the dough well and put it back into the bowl. Cover and leave it to rise for about an hour in a warm place. 3. Put the dough on a flour-covered surface and knead well again. You may add the rest of the flour at this point. Divide the dough into six pieces and roll each piece into a strip about 16 inches long, then wind around a thickish stick. 4. Bake the bread over the embers of a fire, but be careful not to have the bread too close to the heat. The bread will be baked sufficiently when it gives a hollow sound when you knock on it, or when it easily slips off the stick. Baking time depends on the fire and your patience, but usually around ten minutes. HYGGE TIP: CREATE A COOKING CLUB A few years ago, I wanted to create some kind of system that would mean I would get to see some of my good friends on a regular basis, so we formed a cooking club. This was in part prompted by my work, as the importance of our relationships always emerges as a key indicator of why some people are happier than others. Furthermore, I wanted to organize the cooking club in a way that maximized the hygge. So instead of taking turns being the host and cooking for the five or six other people, we always cook together. That is where the hygge is. The rules are simple. Each time there is a theme, or a key ingredient—for example, duck or sausages—each person brings ingredients to make a small dish to fit the theme. It creates a very relaxed, informal, egalitarian setting, where no one person has to cater for the guests—or live up to the standards of the last fancy dinner party. One of the most hyggelig evenings we have had in the cooking club was the time we tried to make sausages. We spent three or four hours mincing the meat, stuffing the casings, boiling and frying the sausages. Feeling proud of ourselves, we were looking at mountains of sausages when we were finally able to sit down, around ten o'clock in the evening, hungry as Vikings. The result: disastrous. The first taste sensation I got was mold. Not exactly what you are looking for in a sausage. We might have gone to bed slightly hungry that night— but the evening had been very hyggelig.*

5
CLOTHING

CASUAL IS KEY When it comes to Denmark, casual is key. Danes in general enjoy a casual tone, a casual atmosphere, and a casual dress code. You will not find many three-piece suits on the streets of Copenhagen, and if you are part of the pinstriped business brigade, you are bound to find the Danish way of dressing almost sloppy. However, you may in time discover that there is a Danish art to master being stylish and casual at the same time. For the casual yet stylish look, many people—including me—go with the combo of a T-shirt or sweater on the inside and then a blazer on the outside. I prefer the ones with leather patches on the elbows for the hygge and for the professor look. In fact, I may overuse the patches a little bit, as my friends joke that if they need to look for me when I am standing with my back to them in a crowded bar, they just look out for the patches. HOW TO DRESS LIKE A DANE Danish fashion is sleek, minimalistic, elegant, but not highly strung. In many ways, it is a sweet spot between hygge and minimalistic functional design. SCARVES A scarf is a must. This goes for men as well as women. While it is predominantly for the winter, people suffering from scarves withdrawal symptoms have been observed wearing scarves midsummer. The golden rule is: the bigger the better. So pile that stylish, thickly wrapped scarf on, just one step short of risking neck injuries. The Danes love scarves so much that some Brits have been referring to the Danish TV drama Borgen as "Scarf Watch." BLACK Once you get out of Copenhagen airport, you may think you have walked onto the set of a ninja movie. In Denmark, everyone wears black. You want to aim for a look that would be fitting for Karl Lagerfeld's funeral: stylish but monochrome. In the summertime, you are allowed to go for a wider range of colors, even something crazily flamboyant like gray. TOP BULKY A combination of hand-knitted wool sweaters, jumpers, cardigans, and pullovers on top, and black leggings for girls and skinny jeans for boys will give you the balance between hygge and fashion. Sweaters can be bulky but never sloppy—and don't forget the scarf. LAYERS The key to surviving four seasons in one day is layers. You should always bring another cardigan. You can't hygge when you are cold. WOOLEN SOCKS Ally yourself with a nice pair of woolen socks as a hygge insurance. CASUAL HAIR The Danish hairstyle is casual to the point of being borderline lazy. Wake up and go. Girls can put their hair in a bun, the higher the better. THE SARAH LUND SWEATER Perhaps the most iconic sweater is the one made famous by Sarah Lund in the Danish TV drama The Killing. The Guardian even featured an article entitled "The Killing: Sarah Lund's jumper explained." The sweater became so popular that the company producing it in the Faroe Islands couldn't keep up with demand. It was the actress Sofie Gråbøl who chose the sweater. "I saw that sweater and thought, that's it! Lund is so sure of herself. She doesn't have to wear a suit. She's at peace with herself." The sweater is also a reminder of her childhood in the seventies and her hippie parents, who wore similar sweaters. "That sweater was a sign of believing in togetherness." HYGGE TIP: HOW TO BUY Link purchases with good experiences. I had saved money for a new favorite chair but waited until I had published my first book to get it. That way, the chair reminds me of something that was an important accomplishment for me. We can apply the same thing to that special sweater or that pair of nice woolen socks. Save for them—but wait until you have that really hyggelig experience: you want to be reminded of it when you pull them on.

6

HOME

HYGGE HEADQUARTERS Danish TV dramas such as *Borgen, The Killing,* and *The Bridge* are, by people abroad, sometimes referred to as "furniture porn." Most scenes are shot in beautifully decorated houses and flats furnished with Danish design classics. And yes, Danes do love design, and walking into many Danish homes can be like walking into the pages of an interior design magazine. The reason for the Danish obsession with interior design is that our homes are the hygge headquarters. Home is central to social life in Denmark. Whereas other countries have a culture of social life predominantly taking place in bars, restaurants, and cafés, Danes prefer *hjemmehygge* (home hygge)—among other reasons, to avoid the high prices charged in restaurants. Seven out of ten Danes say they experience most hygge at home. Danes therefore tend to put a lot of effort and money into making their homes hyggelige. They enjoy the most living space per capita in all of Europe. One December while I was a student, I spent all my spare time selling Christmas trees. It was a cold winter, but working with the trees kept me warm. I spent the entire salary I earned that month from carrying, sawing, hammering, chopping, and selling trees on a chair: the Shell Chair, a beauty designed in 1963 by Hans J. Wegner. Mine was walnut with dark brown leather. Two years later, my apartment was broken into. They stole the chair. Needless to say, I was angry that my beautiful chair had been stolen. But at least the burglars had good taste. Perhaps the Danish obsession with design is best exemplified by what is now known as the Kähler Vase Scandal, or simply Vasegate. The Kähler vase was an anniversary piece that was sold in a limited edition on August 25, 2014. More than 16,000 Danes tried to buy it online that day—most in vain, as the vase quickly sold out. The website crashed and people queued in long lines outside the stores that were stocking the vase. The company that produced the vase was hit by a public backlash over the limited supply.

Was this a little too much hysteria over an eight-inch-high vase with copper stripes, even though it would complement most Danish homes nicely? Perhaps, but Danes have relatively short working weeks, and get free health care and a university education on top of five weeks of paid holiday per year. Not getting that vase was the worst thing that had happened to them in years. HYGGE WISHLIST: TEN THINGS THAT WILL MAKE YOUR HOME MORE HYGELLIG 1. A HYGGEKROG. 2. A FIREPLACE 3. CANDLES 4. THINGS MADE OUT OF WOOD 5. NATURE 6. BOOKS 7. CERAMICS 8. THINK TACTILE 9. VINTAGE 10. BLANKETS AND CUSHIONS 1. A HYGGEKROG The one thing that every home needs is a hyggekrog, which roughly translates as "a nook." It is the place in the room where you love to snuggle up in a blanket, with a book and a cup of tea. Mine is by the kitchen window. I've put some cushions, a blanket, and a reindeer hide there, and I also sit there to work in the evenings. In fact, many of these pages were written there. Danes love their comfy space. Everyone wants one, and hyggekroge are common in Copenhagen and throughout the country. Walking on the streets of the city, you will notice that many of the buildings have a bay window. On the inside, these are almost certainly filled with cushions and blankets, providing the people who live there with a cozy place to sit and relax after a long day. Your hyggekrog does not need to be by the window, however, even though that is really hyggeligt. It could be a part of a room. Just add some cushions or something else that feels nice to sit on, have soft lighting, maybe a blanket, and you will have your own hyggekrog, where you can enjoy a good book and something to drink. To furnish hyggeligt is a big deal in Denmark. Some real estate agents even use a hyggekrog as a way to sell houses. Our love of small spaces may, if we look back in time, go back to when we lived in caves and it was important to pay attention to your environment in order to protect yourself and your group against dangerous animals and other threats. Living in small spaces was preferable, since the warmth generated by the inhabitants' bodies did not disappear as fast as it would in a larger one; in addition, small spaces were great places to hide from predators. Today, one of the reasons we like to sit in a hyggekrog could be that it makes us feel safe; overlooking another room or the street gives us the advantage of spotting any potential threat. We feel relaxed when we're in a hyggekrog. We feel that we have control over our situation and do not feel exposed to the unpredictable. 2. A FIREPLACE I was a fortunate child. My childhood home had an open fireplace and a wood-burning stove. As a kid, my favorite chore was to stack the firewood and light the fire. I am sure I am not the only one. According to the Danish Ministry for the Environment, there are around 750,000 fireplaces and wood-fired stoves in Denmark. With a little over 2.5 million homes in the country, that means that three out of ten homes in Denmark have a hygge advantage. In comparison, around a million homes in the United Kingdom have installed a wood stove, but with a total of 28 million British homes, that's only around one in twenty-eight. In this regard, the US is well-positioned for hygge today. According to the National Association of Home Builders, 60 percent of new homes have at least one fireplace, compared with a third of homes built forty years ago. It is also one of the favorite amenities for potential buyers. So what's the reason for the Danish obsession with burning logs? You've probably already guessed the answer to this one, but surely it can't only be about hygge? Well, according to a study conducted by the University of Aarhus, that is true: Danes have wood-burning stoves because they are considered a cheap heating option, but this is only the second biggest reason for having one. Once again, it's mostly about hygge. Sixty-six percent of all respondents in the study specifically addressed hygge as the most important reason for having a woodburning stove. And if you ask Danes, 70 percent will agree that fireplaces are hyggelig. One respondent to the survey even called fireplaces the most hyggelig piece of applied art ever made. It is fair to say that a fireplace may just be the ultimate headquarters of hygge. It's somewhere we sit by ourselves to rest while experiencing ultimate feelings of coziness and warmth, and it's somewhere we spend time with our dear ones to intensify our feeling of togetherness. 3. CANDLES No candles, no hygge. If this is a surprise to you, you need to revisit Chapter 1. 4. THINGS MADE OUT OF WOOD Maybe we hanker after our roots, but there is just something about wooden things. The smell of burning wood from a fireplace, or even a match, the smooth feeling of a wooden bureau, the soft creak of a wooden floor as you trip across it to have a seat in the wooden chair by the window. Wooden children's toys have become popular again, after years of plastic toys. Kay Bojesen's wooden monkey is an excellent example of this. Wood makes us feel closer to nature; it is simple and natural, just like the concept of hygge. 5. NATURE Wood is not enough. Danes feel the need to bring the entire forest inside. Any piece of nature you might find is likely to get the hygge greenlight. Leaves, nuts, twigs, animal skins . . . Basically, you want to think: How would a Viking squirrel furnish a living room? Be sure to smother those benches, chairs, and windowsills in sheepskin to give them an extra layer of hygge. You may alternate between sheep and reindeer, while keeping cowhides for the floor. With the Danes' love of candles and wooden and other flammable things, it is no surprise that Copenhagen has been burned to the ground on several occasions. Make sure fire precautions are taken. 6. BOOKS Who does not like a shelf filled with thick books? Taking a break with a good book is a cornerstone in the concept of hygge. The genre does not matter—romance, sci-fi, cookbooks, or even horror stories are welcome on the shelves. All books are hyggelig, but classics written by authors such as Jane Austen, Charlotte Brontë, Leo Tolstoy, and Charles Dickens have a special place on the bookshelf. At the right age, your kids may also love to cuddle up with you in the hyggekrog and have you read to them. Probably not Tolstoy, though. 7. CERAMICS A nice teapot, a vase on the dining table, that favorite mug you always want to drink out of—they are all hyggelige. Two of the most iconic Danish ceramics are Kähler, which goes back more than 175 years and made a big impression at the Universal Exposition in Paris in 1889—the year the Eiffel Tower was inaugurated—and of course Royal Copenhagen, founded in 1775 under the protection of Queen Juliane Marie, which has had a revival in popularity in recent years with the Blue Fluted Mega range. 8. THINK TACTILE As you may have discovered by now, a hyggelig interior is not just about how things look, it is just as much about how things feel. Letting your fingers run across a wooden table, over a warm ceramic cup, or through the hairs of the skin of a reindeer is a distinctly different feeling from being in contact with something made from steel, glass, or plastic. Think about the way objects feel to your touch and add a variety of textures to your home. 9. VINTAGE Vintage is a big deal in Danish homes, and you can find pretty much anything in a vintage or antiques shop. Often, the challenge is to find diamonds among a lot of coal. An old lamp, table, or chair is considered really hyggeligt. One can find everything one needs to create a lovely home in a vintage store, and the fact that all the things there have a history makes them even more interesting and hyggelig. With many of these items, narratives and nostalgia come into play. Objects are more than their physical properties; they hold an emotional value and a story. I think my favorite pieces of furniture in my apartment are two footstools. My uncle and I made them together. I am sure I could find something similar in the shops around Copenhagen, but nothing that would mean the same to me. When I look at them, I remember that afternoon ten years ago when we carved them out of a branch of a hundred-year-old walnut tree. That is hygge. They allow you to sit comfortably with your legs up, plus they're made of wood and hold nostalgic value. They are, essentially, the Kinder egg of hygge. 10. BLANKETS AND CUSHIONS Blankets and cushions are must-haves in any hygge household, especially during the cold months of winter. To snuggle up with a blanket is very hyggeligt, and sometimes one does it even though one is not feeling cold, simply because it is cozy. Blankets can be made out of fabrics such as wool or fleece, which are warmer, or cotton for a lighter feeling. Large or small, cushions are also hygge essentials. What is better than leaning your head against a nice cushion while reading your favorite book?

At this point, you are welcome to go Freudian on the Danes and point out that hygge seems to be about comfort food and security blankets. And perhaps you are right. Hygge is about giving your responsible, stressed-out achiever adult a break. Relax. Just for a little while. It is about experiencing happiness in simple pleasures and knowing that everything is going to be okay. HYGGE EMERGENCY KIT You may also consider building a hygge emergency kit, stored up for those evenings when you are low on energy, have no plans, don't feel like going out, and are in the mood for some quality time alone. Have a box, cupboard or suitcase filled with hygge essentials. The list below might give you inspiration as to what you put in it, but of course it is completely up to you to decide and discover what you need for a fast track to hygge. 1. CANDLES 2. SOME GOOD-QUALITY CHOCOLATE Why not visit the closest chocolatier and bring home a little box of highquality chocolate? It doesn't have to be expensive, just a little treat to savor every now and then. If you are like me, make a contract with yourself that you can have one piece per day or per week;—otherwise it tends to disappear rather quickly. Having it as a weekly or daily ritual will give you a little pleasure to look forward to each day. 3. YOUR FAVORITE TEA (Mine is currently rooibos). 4. YOUR FAVORITE BOOK What book makes you forget the world and disappear in between the pages? Find out and put it in the emergency kit for those hygge evenings. If you have a job like mine, where you need to read a lot of stuff and quickly absorb the key points, you may tend to rush through the pages when you finally pick up fiction. We are tempted to turn immediately to the last page of the John le Carré spy novel: "Ah, what do you know? He was a double agent all along." Remember: this is a different kind of reading. Read slowly and see the story play out. My go-to book is A Farewell to Arms by Ernest Hemingway. 5. YOUR FAVORITE FILM OR TV SERIES Mine is Matador (Monopoly), a Danish drama shot almost forty years ago, portraying life in a small town in Denmark from the Great Depression and through the Nazi occupation of Denmark. The series has become part of the modern self-understanding of Danes, and most Danish people will know at least a few of the lines. 6. JAM There is something hyggeligt about jam, especially if you or someone you know has made it. So spend the summer conserving the fruit. Your hygge kit will thank you for it. 7. A GOOD PAIR OF WOOLEN SOCKS 8. A SELECTION OF YOUR FAVORITE LETTERS The spoken word ceases to exist the moment it is born, but with the written language we are able to hear words from centuries ago or the words of loved ones far away. Rereading old letters is a hyggelig way of relaxing, remembering and reconnecting. There is something more hyggeligt about a letter on paper than a letter on a screen. If you grew up in the last century, as I did, you'll have those handwritten letters safely stored away, but letters written in the Internet age may be printed and stored as well. 9. A WARM SWEATER 10. A NOTEBOOK 10. A NOTEBOOK Keep a nice notebook in your hygge emergency kit. We may call this your hygge journal. The first exercise is to note down some of the most hyggelige moments you have experienced in the past month or year. This will allow you to enjoy them again and make you mindful of which experiences you enjoyed. For the second exercise, think of what kind of hyggelige experiences you would like to have in the future. A bucket list of hygge, if you will. 11. A NICE BLANKET 12. PAPER AND A PEN It was nice and hyggeligt to read those old letters, wasn't it? Why not return the favor? Take the time to write a handwritten letter. Think of someone who you are grateful to have in your life and write to them to tell them why. 13. MUSIC Vinyl would be considered more hyggelig than digital, but services like iTunes and Spotify allow you to create a hygge playlist that's up and running. I would go for something slow. Lately, I've been listening a lot to Gregory Alan Isakov and Charles Bradley, but you may want to go with the Danish artist Agnes Obel. 14. A PHOTO ALBUM You know all those photos you uploaded on Facebook? Why not select a hundred of your favorite pictures and have them printed? An album of printed photos is much more hyggelig to browse through on a stormy night with a mug of tea.

7

HAPPY LIVING OUTSIDE THE HOME

looking for patterns in the evidence. So, if we look at cases of hyggelige, we also find some common denominators for these moments of hygge. (I think we have already covered food and candles extensively enough, so we will leave these out for now.) COMPANY You can hygge by yourself. Snuggling up under a blanket with your favorite TV show on a rainy Sunday afternoon is hyggeligt; having a glass of red wine watching a thunderstorm is hyggeligt too, or simply just sitting by the window watching the world go by. But the most hyggelige moments seem to happen in the company of other people. A few years ago, my dad and his two brothers turned two hundred years combined, so they rented a big summer cabin on the west coast of Denmark and invited the whole family. The cabin was surrounded by sand dunes and was set in a rough, rugged landscape where the wind always blows harshly. We spent a weekend there doing nothing but eating, drinking, talking, and walking on the beach. I think that was the most hyggelig weekend I spent all year. CASUALNESS Most hyggelige moments seem to be built on a foundation of casualness. In order for you and your guests to be able to hygge, you need to feel relaxed. There is no need to make things formal. Come as you are and be as you are. When I was in my twenties, I took part in the harvest of grapes one autumn in Champagne. A couple of years ago, I was visiting the region with three friends and we decided to stop by the Marquette vineyard where I had worked. We met Glennie, the lady of the house, and her son, who was by now a fully grown man, and spent a hyggelig afternoon at the vineyard and in the rustic country kitchen, with its low ceiling and flagstones, drinking wine at one of the long tables. The mood of the evening was relaxed and casual; despite the fact that I hadn't seen Glennie and her son for a number of years, there was no need for any formality. CLOSENESS TO NATURE Whether you are sitting by a river in Sweden or in a vineyard in France, or just in your garden or nearby park, being surrounded by nature enables you to bring your guard down and adds a certain simplicity. When we are close to nature, we are not engulfed in entertaining electronics or juggling a broad spectrum of options. There are no luxuries or extravagance, just good company and good conversation. Simple, slow, rustic elements are a fast track to hygge. One summer I went camping with a group of friends along the Nissan River in Sweden. We were roasting chickens over the fire, and they were slowly turning nice and golden. In the fire, you could hear the sizzling of the baking potatoes wrapped in foil. We had paddled a fair distance in the canoes that day, and now darkness was falling. The fire lit up the trees surrounding our camp with warm colors, but despite the light from the fire, you could still see the stars through the treetops. As we waited for the golden chickens to be ready, we drank whiskey out of coffee mugs. We were silent, tired, and happy, and it was pure hygge. BEING IN THE PRESENT MOMENT There is an element of being present in those moments. Hygge is charged with a strong orientation and commitment toward experiencing and savoring the present moment. On that camping trip, there was nowhere else we needed to be. We were off-line. No phone. No e-mail. We were surrounded by nature and good company, and were able to fully relax and take in the moment. Every summer I go sailing with one of my best friends and his dad. There are few things I enjoy more than standing at the helm under full white sails and a blue sky, listening to the music blasting from below deck. The most hyggelige moments on these trips are when we are docked at the various harbors we visit. After every dinner we sit together and watch the sun set from the deck, while we listen to the wind in the rigging of the ships in the harbor and sip our post-dinner Irish coffee. That is hygge. Creating hygge moments may be best achieved by using some of the elements mentioned above. Sometimes you may be able to get all the ingredients in the pot. For me, that happens in summer cabins. In many ways, life in a cabin offers all of the above, and all my favorite childhood memories gravitate toward a small summer cabin my family owned just six miles outside the city, where we would live from May to September. At that time of year, when even the night knows no darkness, my brother and I would enjoy endless days of summer. We would climb trees, catch fish, play football, ride bicycles, explore tunnels, sleep in tree houses, hide under boats on the beach, build dams and forts, play with bows and arrows, and search the forest for berries and hidden Nazi gold. The cabin was a third of the size of our house in the city, the furniture was old, and the TV was black and white and had a fourteen-inch screen and a moody antenna. But this was the place where we had the most hygge. In many ways, these were the happiest times, and the most hyggelige. I think it may be because, in many ways, cabins include all the drivers of hygge: the smells, the sounds, and the simplicity. When you stay in one, there is a closer connection to nature and to each other. A cabin forces you to live more simply and slowly. To get out. To get together. To enjoy the moment. HYGGE DURING OFFICE HOURS However, hygge is not restricted to cozy cabins, Irish coffees on the deck, or snuggling up in your hyggekrog at home in front of the fire. Danes believe that hygge can—and should—happen at the office. Exhibit A in this theory is, of course, the cake discussed in chapter 4. In addition, according to a survey on hygge conducted by the Happiness Research Institute, there is the evidence that 78 percent of Danes say that work should be hyggeligt, too. So, how do you make office hours more hyggeligt? Well, cakes and candles, obviously. But this is just the start. Think of ways to make things more casual, cozy, and egalitarian. Here are five ideas to get the hygge going at the office. 1. ORGANIZE A POTLUCK FRIDAY. Instead of bringing lunch just for yourself, why not organize potlucks for lunch one day of the week? When everybody shares, everybody gets hygge. 2. SET UP AN OFFICE GARDEN. If the office or the surroundings allow it, you can add to the hygge by planting a few plants. Spending a few minutes each day tending to them may be a nice way to manage stress. Extra hygge points if you grow produce that can be enjoyed at lunch. 3. BRING YOUR DOG TO WORK. A few years ago, Michael, one of my interns had to take care of his mother's dog, Leica, for a few weeks and asked whether he could bring her to the office. Best weeks ever. Having Leica at the office definitely increased the hygge and office joy. I made a deal with myself that after accomplishing an item on my to-do list, I could go and pet Leica. My productivity went through the roof. 4. TRY TO MAKE THE OFFICE MORE HOMEY. Could we put in a couple of couches for people to use when they have long reports to read or need to hold a quick and informal meeting? I do a lot of interviews because of my work and I prefer sitting on the couch with the journalist and having a good conversation with them, instead of the two of us facing each other across a fancy table in a sterile office setting. 5. HYGGE CUBICLE LIFE. Maybe you can't change the office, but what about your desk? Could you add some plants, have some hygge socks in the drawer for working in the late evenings? Or go all the way, think of your cubicle as the Batcave of hygge and be the secret hygge hero at the office. The one that leaves a nice piece of chocolate at your colleagues' desks while they are at lunch.

8

HYGGE (HAPPY LIVING) ALL YEAR ROUND

NOT JUST FOR CHRISTMAS In Denmark, a popular saying goes "There is no bad weather, only bad clothing." But, frankly, there are not a lot of great things to say about the weather in Denmark. Some describe the Danish weather as dark, windy, and damp; some say Denmark has two winters, one gray and one green. With this kind of weather, it will come as no surprise that Danes spend most of their time indoors in the winter months. In summertime, most Danes spend as much time as possible outside, desperately hoping to enjoy some sun, but in the months from November to March, the weather forces Danes to stay indoors. As Danes do not have the opportunity to enjoy winter activities in their own country, as in Sweden and Norway, or to spend time outdoors in the winter period, as in southern Europe, all Danes have left to do is hygge at home. As a result, the high season for hygge is autumn and winter, according to a study on hygge conducted by the Happiness Research Institute. Here is a selection of ideas for how to hygge throughout the year. JANUARY: MOVIE NIGHT The month of January is the perfect time to relax with friends and family with a casual movie night. Let each person bring snacks to share, and pick out one of the old classics, one that you've all seen, so it doesn't matter too much if people chat a bit during the film. An entertaining add-on to movie night is to come up with the shortest way of explaining the plot of the given movie. This turns The Lord of the Rings trilogy into "Group spends nine hours returning jewelry" and Forrest Gump into "Drugaddicted girl takes advantage of mentally challenged boy for decades." FEBRUARY: SKI TRIP If you have the opportunity, organize your friends and family to head to the mountains at this time of the year. Yes, the view in the mountains is stunning, the speed on the slopes is exhilarating, and the purity of the air is amazing—but the best part of the ski trip is the hygge. The magic happens when you and your crew get back to your cabin, tired from the slopes, dirty, and messy-haired, and relax with coffee in shared silence. Remember to pack the Grand Marnier! MARCH: THEME MONTH If you and your family are going somewhere on vacation in the summer this might be a way to get a jump on the hygge. If you are going to Spain, spend March exploring the country from afar. By "exploring," I mean watch Spanish movies, make tapas, and if you have kids, maybe spend one evening putting Post-its on the chairs (sillas), table (mesa), plates (platos) in Spanish, so you can get a head start with the language. If you are not going on vacation this year, you can either take the theme from a country you have been to previously (get those photo albums out) or pick your dream destination. If you can't go to the country, bring the country home to you. APRIL: HIKING AND COOKING OVER AN OPEN FIRE April can be a wonderful month to go hiking, camping, or canoeing. Weatherwise, it may be a bit brisk, so remember to pack those woolen socks (they are extra hyggelige), but the month offers benefits in terms of fewer mosquitoes. If you are a city dweller like me, it is natural to panic in the first hours of a hike, thinking, "What the hell will we do out here without Wi-Fi?" However, once you overcome this, your heart rate and stress levels will drop. Hiking is an Easter egg of hygge, as it includes slowness, rusticity, and togetherness. Gather the wood, build the fire, prepare the food, and watch it cook slowly over the fire, then enjoy the after-dinner whiskey with your friends under the stars. Remember to pack the chocolate eggs for the kids if you are heading out for Easter. MAY: WEEKEND CABIN The days are getting longer, and May is the time to start making use of the countryside. One of your friends might have access to a cabin, or you may find a cheap rental—the more rustic the cabin, the more hygge. A fireplace is a bonus. Be sure to pack board games for rainy afternoons. A weekend in May might also present the first opportunity of the year for a barbecue. In terms of summer hygge, nothing beats standing around the grill with a beer in your hand. JUNE: ELDERFLOWER CORDIAL AND THE SUMMER SOLSTICE Early June is the perfect time to harvest elderflowers to make cordial or lemonade. St John's Eve falls on June 23, and on that evening Danes celebrate the summer solstice. This is my favorite tradition. In Denmark, the sun in June sets close to 11 p.m. on a night that never lets go of the light completely. As the sun sets, there is a bittersweet acknowledgment that, from tomorrow, we will start the slow descent into darkness as the days shorten. This is the perfect evening for a picnic. Grab your friends and family and light a bonfire. (They are usually lit relatively late because of the light, so if you need to entertain the kids during the wait, this is a great evening for an egg-and-spoon race.) ELDERFLOWER CORDIAL Whether you drink it cold on a hot summer day or warm during winter, this elderflower cordial will have the smell of summer. And not only when you drink it: to make the cordial you have to leave the flowers and the lemons in a pan for twenty-four hours, so your whole house will smell of summer hygge. Just one whiff immediately transports me back to my childhood summers. For 10½ cups of elderflower lemonade, serves 10–12 30 elderflower clusters 3 large lemons 6 cups water 8 cups sugar 1. Wash elderflower clusters well and place them in a large bowl. 2. Scrub the lemons under hot water, slice them, and add them to the clusters in the bowl. 3. Bring the water to a boil and add the sugar. 4. Pour the hot water into the bowl containing the elderflower clusters and lemon slices. 5. Cover the bowl with a lid and let the lemonade rest for three days. 6. Strain the liquid and pour it into bottles. Store in the fridge. JULY: SUMMER PICNIC July is when Danes really love to get out and enjoy nature. The weather is warm and the evenings are still long. This is the perfect time of year for a picnic by the sea, in a meadow, or in a park. The choice is yours, but get out of town. Invite your family, friends, neighbors, or the people who just moved in down the street. Make it a potluck event, so everybody brings a dish or two to share. Potluck dinners are usually more hyggelig, because they are more egalitarian. They are about sharing food and sharing the responsibility and chores. AUGUST: THE PERSEID METEOR SHOWER Bring blankets for a night under the stars. While the light nights at this time of year may not be the best in which to watch stars, the Perseid meteor shower occurs in mid-August, usually reaching peak activity around the eleventh to the thirteenth. Look northeast for the Perseus constellation, which has Andromeda to the east and Cassiopeia to the north. If you have kids, this is a great time to bring a book of stories from Greek mythology to read while you wait for the shooting stars. For people in the southern hemisphere, the Eta Aquarid meteor shower is an option. It usually peaks between late April and mid-May. SEPTEMBER: MUSHROOM FORAGING Mushrooms appear mainly in the autumn but can be found from late summer on. There is no better taste than food you have grown, caught, or foraged yourself— and it has a high hygge factor. Bring family and friends for a forage excursion to the forest. WARNING: Eating the wrong sort of mushrooms can be deadly, so find an experienced mushroom forager and ask them to come along on a forage. Many communities organize group tours. OCTOBER: CHESTNUTS It is chestnut season. If you have kids, take them chestnut hunting and use the chestnuts to make animal figurines. For the adults, buy edible chestnuts, make a cross with a knife in the pointy end, and roast them in the oven at 200 degrees for about thirty minutes, until the skins open and the insides are tender. Peel off the tough outside skin and add a bit of butter and salt. If you just want quality hygge time by yourself, pick up some mandarins, roasted chestnuts, and a copy of A Moveable Feast by Hemingway. It is set in 1920s Paris, when Hemingway was working as a penniless writer. NOVEMBER: SOUP COOK-OFF Winter is coming. It is time to get out the old soup recipes and find new ones. Invite family and friends over for a soup cook-off. Each person brings ingredients for a soup to feed one person. Take turns preparing small dishes of different soups, enough for everyone to try. I usually make a pumpkin-ginger soup, which works really well with a bit of crème fraîche. If you want to do something extra as host, bake some homemade bread. The smell of freshly baked bread is definitely hygge. DECEMBER: GLØGG AND ÆBLESKIVER (PANCAKE PUFFS) This is hygge high season. The consumption of candles and confectionery soars, as do BMIs. This is also prime time for gløgg (you'll find the recipe in Chapter 4). Start out well in advance by soaking those raisins in port and invite your friends and family over for an afternoon or evening of gløgg and æbleskiver (recipe in Chapter 11).

9

HYGGE ON THE CHEAP

THE BEST THINGS IN LIFE ARE FREE *There is nothing fancy, expensive, or luxurious about a pair of ugly woolen hygge socks—and that is a vital feature of the anatomy of hygge. Champagne and oysters may be many things, but hygge is not one of them. Hygge is humble and slow. It is choosing rustic over new, simple over posh and ambience over excitement. In many ways, hygge might be the Danish cousin to slow and simple living. It is wearing your pajamas and watching Lord of the Rings the day before Christmas, it is sitting in your window watching the weather while sipping your favorite tea, and it is looking into the bonfire on summer solstice surrounded by your friends and family while your twistbread slowly bakes. Simplicity and modesty are central to hygge, but they are also considered virtues when it comes to Danish design and culture. Simplicity and functionality are the main ingredients of Danish design classics, and the Danes' love affair with modesty means that bragging about your accomplishments and flashing your Rolex are not only frowned upon and considered poor taste, but spoil the hygge. In short, the more bling, the less hygge. Consequently, you can also play the hygge card as an exit strategy if you enter a high-end restaurant you can't afford. "Shouldn't we find a place that is more hyggeligt?" is a perfectly valid reason to find a cheaper establishment. Not Noma, though. That restaurant is really hyggeligt. It has the right lighting. Hygge is about appreciating the simple pleasures in life and can be achieved on a shoestring budget. The poem and song "The Happy Day of Svante" by Benny Andersen is famous in Denmark. It's all about savoring the moment and enjoying simple pleasures: "Look, real daylight soon. Red sun and waning moon. She takes a shower for me. Me whom it's good to be. Life's not bad, for it's all we have got. And the coffee's almost hot." Okay, so Danes might be better at hygge than poetry, but one of the most consistent patterns in happiness research is how little*

39

difference money makes. Of course, if you can't afford to eat, money is of the utmost importance, but if you're not battling poverty or struggling to make ends meet, an additional $100 per month is not going to move the needle when it comes to happiness. This fits well with hygge. You cannot buy the right atmosphere or a sense of togetherness. You cannot hygge if you are in a hurry or stressed out, and the art of creating intimacy cannot be bought by anything but time, interest, and engagement in the people around you. Hygge can and often will be about eating or drinking, but the more it counteracts consumption, the more hyggeligt it is. The more money and prestige is associated with something, the less hyggeligt it becomes. The simpler and more primitive an activity is, the more hyggeligt it is. Drinking tea is more hyggeligt than drinking champagne, playing board games is more hyggeligt than playing computer games, and home-cooked food and biscuits are more hyggeligt than store-bought ones. In short, if you want hygge, there is no amount of money that you can spend which will increase the hygge factor—at least not if you are buying anything more expensive than a candle. Hygge is an atmosphere that is not only unimproved by spending more money on it, but rather, in some ways, the opposite. Hygge may be bad fort capitalism, but it may prove to be very good for your personal happiness. Hygge is appreciating the simple pleasures in life and can be achieved with very little money. Here are ten examples how the best hygge in life is free—or almost so.
TEN INEXPENSIVE HYGGE ACTIVITIES 1. BRING OUT THE BOARD GAMES We live in the age of Netflix, Candy Crush, and an endless supply of electronic entertainment. We hang out with technology instead of with each other. However, playing board games is still popular—in part because of the hygge. Every year, my friend Martin organizes the mother of board games: a game of Axis & Allies. Set in World War II, it is essentially a complex version of the game Risk. The game usually lasts for about fourteen hours, and Martin usually leaves his very understanding girlfriend in a hotel for the night. We make the evening into more than simply playing a game. There'll be classical music on—mostly Wagner and Beethoven— and smoke from cigars fills the room, so you can barely see our group of grown men in uniforms. Admittedly, we may take it to an extreme level, but we do it for the hygge. But why are board games hygge? Well, first of all, it is a social activity. You play games together. You create common memories and strengthen bonds. All of Martin's friends still remember the moment in the 2012 game when the Allies suddenly realized that Moscow would fall. In addition, for many of us who grew up with Monopoly or Trivial Pursuit, board games are full of nostalgia and take us back to simpler times. There is also a slowness to the activity (especially if the game takes fourteen hours), a tangibility,

and an air of hygge. 2. PANTRY PARTY This is one of my favorites. Invite your friends over to your house for an afternoon or an evening of cooking and hygge. The rules are simple. Every person brings ingredients to make something that goes in the pantry (or in the fridge). Strawberry jam, sweet pickle relish, ketchup, chicken stock, limoncello, pumpkin soup—you name it. Everybody also brings jars, cans, bottles, or containers in a shape that will allow them to store a bounty of homemade treats. The beauty of it is the diversity. Instead of having ten servings of pumpkin soup, you now have mango chutney, ginger beer, pickled chili, baba ghanoush, a loaf of sourdough bread, plum marmalade, elderflower cordial, walnut aquavit, and raspberry sorbet. Yum. 3. TV NIGHT One of my best friends and I always watch Game of Thrones together. Every two weeks or so, we watch two episodes. No more. I know it is borderline Amish in the age of Netflix not to binge-watch a whole season of your favorite show once it is released, but this approach has some advantages. First, it brings TV back to being something more sociable. Second, it allows you to look forward to something on a regular basis. So restrain yourself from bingeing and invite friends over for weekly viewings of a specific TV show. 4. CROQUET Playing croquet is a great way of hanging out with family and friends. The game is informal and slow, so it allows for conversation at the same time and there is something to watch while you talk. Find the nearest park or a yard with a stretch of grass you can use as a croquet field, and bring blankets and a picnic basket. 5. SET UP A MINI-LIBRARY An inexpensive and sustainable way to make a shared space (in your apartment building or neighborhood) a little bit more hyggeligt is to build a small library. Find a rustic dresser or some shelves and put them in the hallway or on the stairway landing (you may want to ask for permission first). Put a handful or more of the books you have already read in the library, but let your neighbors help you increase the selection of titles by following the principle of leaving a book whenever you take one. Being greeted with a display of books when you come into your building is a more hyggelig way of returning home. Also, it may encourage more hygge interaction among the tenants. 6. MAKE A FIRE A fire is definitely part of the hygge equation and so is the slow preparation of very unfussy food, but also involved is the togetherness around the fire, the fact that there is no need to keep the conversation going because you have the sound of the fire. Now the fire has burned down and the embers are ready. You have found a suitable straight stick and stripped the bark from the end. Wrap the bread tightly around the stick and place it over the glowing embers. People are gathered in a close circle around the fire now, moving around a little as the smoke changes direction. Your eyes hurt from the smoke, your hand hurts from being close to the fire, and your bread is turning black on the outside yet remaining unbaked on the inside. But it doesn't get any more hyggelig than this. 7. OUTDOOR MOVIES Many cities offer outdoor film screenings during the summer. In Copenhagen, they take place during August, as in June and July it is simply too bright in the evenings to show movies. The sound is usually difficult to hear, you sit kind of uncomfortably on the ground, without back support, and the people who were smart enough to bring small chairs set up camp right in front of you and thus block some of your view of the screen. However, it is still total hyggeligt. I often go with a couple of friends. We set up camp, eat some food, drink some wine, talk, and wait for the movie to start. 8. SWAP PARTY Remember that lamp you have in your basement and have been meaning to put on eBay for two years now? Or that extra blender you and your partner now have since you decided to move in together? Why not get rid of it by swapping it for something that you do need—and have a hyggelig evening at the same time? Invite friends and family over for a swap party. The rules are simple. Each person brings something he or she doesn't use anymore that could be of value to someone else. Beyond being wallet-and ecofriendly, it is also a nice opportunity to clean out your wardrobe, kitchen cabinet, basement, or wherever you store the things you never use. Furthermore, it may be more convenient and fun to swap with friends than to spend a weekend pushing your junk at the flea market or posting a listing. 9. SLEDDING In the wintertime, it is easy to feel stuck inside. And while it can be hyggeligt to relax with your book and a cup of tea, it is even more hyggeligt after you have spent a day in the snow. So gather a group of people and head for the hills. If you have a beautiful wooden sleigh stashed in the basement, great, but cheaper options exist. You can use a sturdy plastic bag to sleigh down a hill. Sledding is free and fun. Bring a winter picnic basket with tea or mulled wine for afterward. Don't drink and sled. 10. PLAY In many ways, some of the activities above, like sledding and board games, fall into the same category—play. We loved them when we were kids but for some reason we stop doing them when we become grown-ups. Adults are not supposed to play. We are supposed to stress, worry, and be too busy dealing with life's problems. But according to a study undertaken by Princeton University and led by Alan Krueger, professor in economics and public affairs there, we are happiest when we are involved in engaging leisure activities. One of our issues as adults is that we become too focused on the results of an activity. We work to earn money. We go to the gym to lose weight. We spend time with people to network and further our careers. What happened to doing something just because it's fun? Notice in the table that follows how social activities such as sports, hiking, partying, and playing with children are the top scorers.

10
HYGGE SAFARI

If you should visit Copenhagen, you might want to visit some of these hyggelige places. NYHAVN (NEW HARBOR) This used to be a dodgy part of town with rowdy sailors and "ladies of pleasure." Today you can visit one of the many restaurants for a pickled herring and schnapps. If that is not your thing, and if the weather is nice, do like the locals and buy a few beers from a shop, have a seat at the bulwark, and watch the city go by. LA GLACE Dive into the cream. Remember the importance of cakes? If there were a Camino de Santiago for cake, La Glace would be the Santiago de Compostela Cathedral. La Glace was established in 1870 and is the oldest confectionery shop in Denmark. TIVOLI GARDENS The Tivoli Gardens were founded in 1843 and are a classic attraction in Copenhagen, where many citizens purchase annual passes to the gardens. While many people visit during the summer, the best time for hygge is when Tivoli dresses up for Christmas and New Year's Eve (usually from mid-November until January). This is a celebration of light. Several hundred thousand lights turn the garden into a magical place in the winter darkness, and you can enjoy some gløgg near one of the bonfires in the garden or get warm by the fireplace at Nimb Bar. ROWBOAT IN CHRISTIANSHAVN ROWBOAT IN CHRISTIANSHAVN Christianshavn is part of the city center in Copenhagen but it is separated from the rest of the center by the Inner Harbor. It is dominated by canals and may remind you a little of Amsterdam. The best way to experience this part of town is by renting a rowboat and rowing along the canals. Bring blankets, wine, and a picnic basket. GRÅBRØDRETORV Being surrounded by the old houses here will transport you back centuries. This hyggelige square gets its name from the monastery of the Grey Brothers (Grå brødre), established in 1238. There are plenty of cozy restaurants in the square. At Peder Oxe you can get classical Danish smørrebrød and enjoy the fireplace. Even one of the hairdressing salons has a fireplace (and a French bulldog, who will happily sleep on your lap while you have your hair cut). Total hygge. You might also be lucky enough to see a full pig roast at the square. VÆRNEDAMSVEJ At Værnedamsvej, cars zigzag between cyclists and pedestrians. This short street will make you slow down and smell the flowers and the coffee. Florists, cafés, wine bars, and interior design shops make this a wonderful place to spend a lazy and hyggelig afternoon. A SMØRREBRØD PLACE Smørrebrød means, literally, spread bread. It is an open sandwich on rye bread. Danes are huge fans of rye bread, so it is usually one of the first things they miss when they are living abroad. Some expats living in Denmark will, however, refer to the bread as the devil's sandals, as they really dislike the taste and find the bread tough to chew. In all regards, smørrebrød is a truly Danish lunch experience. Smørrebrød can have an almost limitless number of toppings, from herring to raw beef, egg, and seafood, and some have colorful names like "the veterinarian's night food." Smørrebrød is usually served with beer and schnapps. In Copenhagen, you will find many traditional smørrebrød places, and such a lunch will surely get the hygge going. LIBRARY BAR In the Plaza Hotel, near the central train station, you will find the Library Bar, which opened in 1914. Here are sofas, wooden panels, leather-bound books, and really hyggelig lighting. The bar features live music from time to time, but on a quiet night it is well suited for deep conversation. If you visit during Christmas, you will find a Christmas tree hanging upside down from the ceiling.

11

IT'S THE MOST HYGGELIG TIME OF YEAR

For many people—Danes included—Christmas is a wonderful time. However, wonderful is far from the only word used to describe it. If you ask people of any nationality to describe Christmas in one word, adjectives like happy, cheerful, warm, and heartfelt would probably surface. Danes would agree with a lot of these. But, they would object, "the most fitting word is missing. You forgot hyggelig!" In Denmark, in one month of the year, the days are so short you will be lucky to catch a glimpse of the sun. Riding your bike to and from work in the cold and wet and in complete darkness, you begin to question why anybody ever thought that settling in Denmark would be a good idea. Yes, I know, in Denmark it is not −30 degrees outside, nor are we troubled with hurricanes or tsunamis. But living here, you do get the sense that the weather gods have taken a certain disliking to the Danes; that they want us to feel miserable and uncomfortable at least one month a year. As unlikely as it sounds, this is the season of hygge in Denmark. Danes simply will not let the weather or the laws of nature define their emotional well-being. Therefore, instead of going into hibernation—which does indeed seem appealing on damp December mornings—Danes have decided to make the best of things. Even though it is possible to hygge all year round, only once a year is hygge the ultimate goal of an entire month. Without achieving hygge, a Dane's toil for the Christmas project is redundant. Chestnuts, a fireplace, friends, and family coming together around a table of delicious treats; decorations of red, green, and gold; the fresh scent of pine from the Christmas tree; carols everybody knows; and the broadcasting of the very same TV shows as last year—and every year before that—these are features of a fairly ordinary Christmas all over the world. From Dallas to Durban, people sing along to the words of "Last Christmas." From Dublin to Dubai, people know the plot of A Christmas Carol. This is no less true in Denmark. Indeed, there are Christmas traditions which are specifically Danish, but a Danish Christmas is not considerably different from a German, French, or British one in terms of activities or traditions. What is different in Denmark, though, is that a Danish Christmas will always be planned, thought of, and evaluated in relation to the concept of hygge. At no other time of the year will you hear Danes mentioning hygge as much. It is literally mentioned at any given opportunity. And, of course, Danish includes a compound word, julehygge (Christmas hygge), which is both an adjective and a verb. "Do you want to come over for some julehygge?" In the pages that follow, I will try to outline a recipe for a proper hyggelig Christmas—a perfect Danish Christmas—which is in itself a daunting task. Danes hold their Christmas dear, and I am sure a lot of Danes will disagree with the elements of Christmas I am going to mention. However, most will probably recognize more than one element from their own traditions. FAMILY AND FRIENDS Every year in the second half of December, a full-blown migration takes place in Denmark. People originally from other parts of Denmark who usually live in Copenhagen pack their stuff, plus tons of presents, and jump on a train headed toward their hometown. A hyggelig Christmas begins and ends with family and friends. Those are the people we feel safe around, the ones who make us feel comfortable. They know us, and we enjoy spending time with them because we love them. Time and time again, the quality of our social relations has been shown to be one of the best predictors for our emotional well-being. In our everyday lives, many of us feel we see too little of our loved ones. Christmas is an opportunity to make up for that; to gather around a table full of delicious treats in order to enjoy life and one another's company. That is the key ingredient in a hyggelig Christmas. People all over the world do the very same each year, but only in Danish homes do people draw a collective sigh of relief when someone reassures the others that "This is hyggeligt." In that moment, both hosts and guests feel that Christmas has arrived; the proper spirit of hygge has been achieved. But family is not enough in order to put together a hyggelig Christmas. Even though a lot of people see friends and family mostly during the holidays, this can be done all year round. TRADITIONS FOOD Around Christmastime, certain rituals and traditions must be adhered to in order to achieve hygge. A Danish Christmas needs the proper decorations, food, and activities in order to be considered a "real" hyggelig Christmas. First, there is the food. Danish food. Heavy Danish food. If you search the Internet for long enough, I am convinced you will find diets that include almost everything. There are diets where you eat only meat or only fat, water diets, diets with lots of carbs and diets without any. There are diets of vegetables and even diets of sunlight. Nonetheless, I have yet to come across a diet that would accept Danish Christmas food. The main protagonist in the Christmas menu is the meat, which is either roast pork or duck—often both. It will be accompanied by boiled potatoes, or caramelized potatoes, stewed sweet-and-sour red cabbage, gravy, and pickled gherkins. Some have cream-stewed cabbage, sausages, and various types of bread, too. To complete the feast, we have a truly Danish invention: risalamande (it comes from the French ris à l'amande, and this makes it sound fancier) is half partwhipped cream, half part-boiled rice, with finely chopped almonds and topped with hot cherry sauce. Eating risalamande is not just a delicious experience, though. It is very much social. Because hidden in the big bowl of dessert is one whole almond. Usually, when everybody has been served a bowl of risalamande, a silence spreads across the room. Eyes shift from person to person. It is more similar to a poker game or a Western-style shootout than a Christmas tradition. "Who's got the almond?" Whoever finds it gets a present and will be the subject of comments about always being lucky (and, somehow it does actually seem that some people are better at getting the almond than others). Soon the silence is replaced by questions: "You've got the almond, haven't you?," "You're hiding it, just like last year, aren't you?" The aim of the one who has found the almond is to hide it and deny having found it in order to lure the others into eating everything in their bowl: it becomes a kind of perverted eating contest. Around Christmastime, eating a dessert turns into a hyggelig social activity in itself. Do you think it sounds delicious? You should taste it. Fortunately for our bodies, we only get to feast on these dishes once a year.

DECORATIONS No hyggelig Christmas is complete without the proper decorations. These may vary even more than the food, as every family has inherited its own decorations from parents and grandparents. But they may include figures of nisse (an elf or gnome), animals, and Father Christmas, mini-nativity figures and cornets or woven hearts made of glossy paper. Woven paper hearts are rarely seen outside Denmark. Their origin has been attributed to Hans Christian Andersen, who was a master at paper cuttings. They're made out of two double-layered cutouts of glossy paper, and the flaps of the two cutouts are woven together to make the heart shape. They come in various colors and have different motifs, and every Dane knows how to craft at least a simple one. (See the section "How to Make Woven Hearts" later in this chapter.) Then there are candles (of course). When 100 percent of the time spent at home in December is during the hours of darkness, you need various sources of lighting, and candles are hyggelige. A specific Danish version of a Christmas candle is the advent candle, painted like a tape measure with dates from December 1 to December 24. Each day the corresponding piece of candle is burned away. However, few people light the calendar candle when they are on their own. Rather, it is done either in the morning, when parents are frantically trying to get everybody ready for school and work, or in the evening, when darkness has spread again and the family is assembled around the dinner table. The calendar light is literally the centerpiece of the family. It constitutes a natural point and time marker to assemble around. And besides, it feeds the Danes' fetish for the countdown to Christmas. COUNTDOWN TO HYGGE The advent candle is not the only way Danes count down to the ultimate hygge day of the year. Danish children have advent calendars and open a flap each day to unveil a Christmas symbol or motif. A more extravagant version is a series of boxes of wood or cardboard, each of which contains, say, a small Christmas bauble or a sweet. Some families even have present calendars and children get a small present each day until Christmas —when they will get even more. And then there are the TV calendars. They are mostly for kids and provide a hyggelig activity to make their wait for the big day tolerable. Every year, most TV stations have their own julekalender—a story usually related to Christmas with twenty-four connected episodes, reaching a climax on December 24, when the adults are busy with last-minute preparations. Emphasizing that Christmas really is the time for hygge, one of the recurring characters in these shows is Lunte, a nisse, who usually greets people by saying, "Hyggehejsa" (hygge hello). A new TV calendar is produced every year, and there is always an old one that is being shown again. And while children are laughing and having a good time watching these shows, you will often find the adults snatching glimpses of the screen and smiling to themselves, reminiscing about being a child and watching the very same scenes while waiting for the coming of Christmas Day. Naturally, these things are in themselves hyggelige. But they are also important because they are traditions. And traditions matter to hygge. Traditions remind us of all the other good times we have had with family and friends. We feel there is a part of Christmas or hygge hidden in these actions and items that have been part of our whole life. Without them, something is missing. Christmas just would not be the same. THE RACE TO RELAX Getting a bit out of breath reading about all the necessities for a Danish Christmas? I completely get it. All the things I have sketched out here do contribute to the pressure for hygge around Christmas. If people are not feeling the hygge, something is not right. Christmas is deemed a failure. All the preparations for a hyggelig Christmas are quite often stressful and, indeed, not very hyggelige. Now, this may seem a bit contradictory, but it actually makes sense. Hygge is possible only if it stands in opposition to something which is not hygge. It is essential for the concept of hygge that it constitutes an alternative to everything that is not hyggeligt in our everyday lives. For a brief moment, hygge protects us against that which is not hyggeligt. There must be anti-hygge for hygge to be valuable. Life might seem stressful. It might seem unsafe and unfair. Life is often centered on money and social status. But life is none of these things in moments of hygge. Remember my friend who commented that the only way our time in the cabin could be more hyggelig was if a storm broke outside? This is hygge. The more it sets the here and now apart from the tough realities of the outside world, the more valuable it becomes. In this way, achieving hygge would not be possible without all the bustle and turmoil leading up to Christmas. All the money, stress, work, and time being sacrificed in the preparations for Christmas leads up to hygge as a climax. Hygge is postponed in order to be accomplished. Knowing friends and family have worked hard all December in order to get together and not focus on work, money, and all things profane is the meaning of hygge. But Christmas still includes moments that threaten to compromise hygge. As hygge is about letting go of the everyday, the focus on, for example, money and the giving and exchanging of presents always threatens to contaminate the pure and pristine hygge. Giving and receiving presents may cause someone to feel exposed or emphasize differences in status. Receiving too big a gift makes you feel in debt to the giver, while giving too big a gift is frowned upon, as it asserts the giver's superior position. Demonstrations of power are not welcome in hygge. In Denmark, Christmas hygge is egalitarian. It is about relations and community, not individuals trying to draw attention to themselves. It is not possible to achieve hygge if anybody feels excluded or superior to anybody else. Therefore, the best Christmases are the ones where everything outlined in this chapter is achieved and where the danger element of gift-giving is eliminated by striking a balance between giving and receiving. Fortunately, once the presents have been exchanged, there are plenty of gift-free, hyggelige days of relaxation and lunches until New Year's Eve, when hygge is again sacrificed so that even more preparations can be made. ÆBLESKIVER (EH-BLEH-SKI-VER) A traditional Danish treat for the Christmas holidays is æbleskiver. Don't forget to serve it with gløgg—(see the recipe for gløgg in Chapter 4). For this you need a special pan—an æbleskiver pan—which can be found and ordered online. Serves 4–6. Cooking time 45 minutes (including 30 minutes rest for the dough) 3 eggs Scant 2 cups buttermilk 2 cups flour 1 tablespoon sugar ¼ teaspoon salt ½ teaspoon baking soda 3 tablespoons melted butter 3 tablespoons melted butter confectioner's sugar, to serve jam, to serve 1. Mix egg yolks, buttermilk, flour, sugar, salt, and baking soda together well. Cover the mixture and let it rest for thirty minutes. 2. Once the mixture has risen, whip the egg whites until stiff and fold gently into the mixture. 3. Heat the æbleskiver pan and put a little butter in each hole. Pour some of the mixture into each hole, filling them three-quarters full and cook over a medium heat. Turn the æbleskiver frequently, so they are cooked evenly. This usually takes five to six minutes. Make the first turn when they have formed a brown crust at the bottom but the dough on top is still runny, using a knitting needle or skewer. 4. Serve them hot with confectioner's sugar and your favorite jam. HYGGE TIP: GET KNITTING Why might someone have a knitting needle laying around? Because knitting is extremely hygge. It is a sign of "everything is safe"–it has a certain grandma vibe to it—and even the sound of knitting is hygge. Knitting also brings calmness to the situation and atmosphere. In fact, one of my friends is currently studying to be a midwife. She and her class were told by one of the professors that they should take up knitting because it would have a calming effect on people in the room when the babies were being delivered. Most of the students in the class were knitting during the next class. Oh, and of course, there are bonus hygge points for socks and scarves you've knitted yourself. CHRISTMAS WOVEN HEARTS There is a long tradition in Denmark for making pleated hearts out of paper as ornaments for the Christmas tree. The origin of the tradition is unknown, but the oldest known heart was in fact made by Hans Christian Andersen in 1860. It is still kept in a museum. In the early twentieth century, making Christmas hearts became widespread, particularly perhaps because pleating the hearts out of glossy paper was considered to improve children's fine motor skills. Today families with kids will spend a healthy part of Sunday afternoons in December making Christmas hearts. HOW TO MAKE WOVEN HEARTS What you need: Two different-colored sheets of glossy paper (here, red and blue), a pair of scissors, a pencil, and a bit of patience. STEP 1: Fold the colored sheets of glossy paper in half. (If the paper is colored on only one side, make sure the colored side faces outward.) On the outer side of each folded piece of paper, draw an outline of the U shape with 4 cut lines (one heart X and one heart Y). The straight edge of the U shape should be along the fold of the paper. STEP 2: Cut out the shapes including along the cut lines. You will have one cutout of each color. Each cutout will have two layers of paper and five flaps. STEP 3: There are only two possible actions when pleating the flaps: a flap either goes through the middle of another flap or has another flap going through the middle of it. Adjacent flaps alternate, so if one flap goes through another, the adjacent flap will do the opposite. To create the woven heart, flap 1 of the blue cutout is threaded through the middle of flap E of the red cutout; flap D is threaded through flap 1;

flap 1 through flap C; flap B through flap 1; and flap 1 through flap A. Repeat this process starting with flap 2 but reverse the process beginning by threading flap E through flap 2. Flap 3 must then be threaded like flap 1; flap 4 like flap 2; and flap 5 like flaps 3 and 1. When flap 5 has been woven through flap A the heart is complete. You are now a qualified Dane!

12
SUMMER HYGGE

———❦———

THE LIVING IS EASY While summer may not encourage the use of candles and fireplaces, summer can be hyggelig, too. Summer is the smell of new-mown grass, suntanned skin, sunscreen, and salt water. It is reading in the shadow of a tree, enjoying the long summer nights, and standing around the barbecue with your friends. Summer doesn't mean you have to turn down the hygge. It is just a different kind of hygge from that of autumn or winter. It involves making use of the sun and the warmth and nature, but summer hygge still builds on the key elements of togetherness and good food. Here are five suggestions you can use to get the hygge going during summer. 1. THINK CIDER HOUSE RULES There are few things more hyggelig than spending a day in an orchard picking fruit. About once a year, my friends and I go to Fejø, a small island in the southern part of Denmark known for its apples. There are rows and rows of apple and plum trees. If we hit the island late in the summer, the Opal plums are ripe and the Filippa apples are ready. Spending one day at the orchard allows you to hygge another day by making jams or preserving the fruit you picked in other ways. This year, I hope we can have a go at making cider. Maybe it's time for that pantry party we talked about earlier. There are many pick-your-own farms scattered throughout the countryside in the UK, US, Canada, Australia, and New Zealand. 2. THROW A BARBECUE FOR FAMILY AND FRIENDS Nothing gets the hygge going faster than lighting the barbecue. This is a type of hygge practiced in most parts of the world. Invite your friends and family over and get cooking together. Light the barbecue, and while you wait for the coals to get to just the right temperature, have a game of croquet. 3. JOIN OR BUILD A COMMUNITY GARDEN At the moment, community gardens seem to be popping up everywhere, and with good reason. They are a wonderful way of getting the hyggelig atmosphere of a village into a bigger city. Tending to your tomatoes while having a chat with other gardeners is both hyggelig and meditative. In addition, it brings people in the local neighborhood together and fosters the development of community spirit. What's not to like? Building community gardens was one of the proposals recommended by the Happiness Research Institute when we were working with a town just outside Copenhagen, trying to come up with ideas that would improve the social fabric and reduce isolation and loneliness in the community. But it was such a great idea that I thought we should build one ourselves. So we did. Across the street from our office is a church that has space for around twenty raised plant beds. We ordered seven tons of dirt and spent one Sunday afternoon building the garden, and of course, to top off the hygge, we finished the day with a barbecue. 4. PICNICS BY THE BEACH Summer is a wonderful time of year to go to your local farmers' market and fill your basket with strawberries, cherries, and watermelon. Add some bread and cheese to the basket, and you're good to go. Bring all your friends, or just that one special person, and find a spot near the sea. This is the recipe for one of the most hyggelig activities you can do throughout the summer. A whole day can easily pass just in talking, reading, and enjoying the freedom of not having to do anything. 5. CARGO BIKE AROUND What better way to experience your city or neighborhood than by cycling around it? Of course, being from Copenhagen, I might be biased in this regard. So if you have the good fortune—as I do—to know some good people who own a cargo bike, you might be able to borrow it for a day. A cargo bike is a bicycle that allows you to have a passenger or two. A threewheeled bicycle with a large box in front for transporting your kids, your spouse, dog, groceries or whatever you want to take for a ride. Of course, you could walk or drive. But the cargo bike can be turned into a movable fortress of hygge. Bring pillows, a blanket, treats, music, a picnic basket—whatever tickles your fancy. This is the perfect way to spend a summer afternoon, but if you add an extra warm blanket and a good sweater, this can also work as a yearround activity. In fact one winter, I biked a beautiful Swedish woman around under the Copenhagen Christmas lights in an attempt to woo her. The attempt failed. "The timing wasn't right" (which I believe translates into "I'm just not that into you" in every language), but I am sure it wasn't because she thought our date lacked hygge. BIKES AND HAPPINESS In addition to hygge, Hans Christian Andersen, Lego, and Danish design, Denmark is known for its love of bikes. Of course, it is easy to be a nation of cyclophiliacs when the country's highest point is less than six hundred and fifty-six feet and when the city invests heavily in infrastructure for cyclists. (Car taxes of 150 to 180 percent probably also help.) Nevertheless, Danes love their bikes and cycling. In Copenhagen, 45 percent of those who live, study, or work in the city cycle to their place of education or employment. Roughly a third of those working in the city but living outside it choose to commute by bicycle. I think most of us appreciate that cycling is an easy way to weave a bit of exercise into our daily routine and is environmentally (and wallet) friendly. However, that is not why Copenhageners bike. We do it because it is easy and convenient. It is simply the fastest way to get from A to B. But there is an additional advantage that may be overlooked and underappreciated: biking makes people happier. A comprehensive study carried out in 2014 by researchers at the University of East Anglia's Norwich Medical School and the Center for Health Economics at the University of York, and based on nearly 18,000 adult commuters over eighteen years, found that people who bike to work are happier than those who drive or use public transport. You might argue that we can't be sure that it's the cycling that causes the happiness. It could just as well be the other way round—that the happier people are, the more inclined they are to cycle. True, but this is where it gets interesting. When the researchers of the study analyzed the results, they discovered that the people who over the years had changed from commuting by car or bus to cycling or going on foot became happier after the switch. And to further bombard you with compelling arguments to give the bike a try, another study, from McGill University in Montreal, also found that those who cycled to work were most satisfied with their commute, even though it could make their commute longer. And if happiness isn't enough of a motivation, let me tell you that according to a Dutch (cyclophiliacs as well) study undertaken by the University of Utrecht, switching from driving to riding a bike in your daily commute adds three to fourteen months to your life expectancy, and a Danish study concluded— perhaps unsurprisingly—that children who cycled to school were significantly fitter than those who were driven. "Okay," you might say. "So cycling will make me healthier and happier. But what good are health and happiness? They can't bring me money . . ." Well, you might not be the ideal target group for my next argument, but here goes: if you bike, we all win. It is good for the community. Cycling is not only beneficial for the individual and his or her well-being and health, but it's an indicator of the degree of neighbors' and locals' sense of community. A Swedish study of 2012 of more than 21,000 people found that people who traveled by car generally attended fewer social events and family gatherings. Furthermore, the drivers had comparatively less trust in other people. Those who chose to walk or cycle to their destinations attended more social events and had a comparatively greater trust in others. This doesn't mean that swapping your car for a bike will instantly improve how much you trust other people. The researchers behind the study point toward the increase in commuting distance as an explanation. Because of a more flexible and accessible labor market, people find jobs farther afield. In turn, this means that people's social networks are spread farther geographically, which reduces their sense of belonging and engagement in their neighborhood. In other words, if a city is designed in a way that makes a long drive to work necessary, we harm the social health of that city. If a lot of people cycle, it's probably an indication that you live in a healthy neighborhood. This is something that should be seriously considered in urban planning if we want to ensure neighborliness and trust among locals.

13

THE TASTE OF HYGGE

Taste is an important element of hygge because it often involves eating something. And that something cannot be too fresh, alternative or challenging in any way. The taste of hygge is almost always familiar, sweet, and comforting. If you want to make a cup of tea more hyggelig, you add honey. If you want to make a cake more hyggelig, you add icing. And if you want your stew to be more hyggelig, you add wine. THE SOUND OF HYGGE The small sparks and dynamic crackles of burning wood are probably the most hyggelige sounds there are. But don't worry if you live in an apartment and cannot have an open fire without also facing great risk of death. Many sounds can be hyggelige. Actually, hygge mainly has to do with the absence of sounds, which enables you to hear even very quiet noises such as raindrops on the roof, wind blowing outside the window, the sound of trees waving in the wind, or the creaks of wooden planks that yield when you walk on them. Also, the sounds of a person drawing, cooking, or knitting could be hyggelig. Any sound of a safe environment will be the soundtrack of hygge. For example, the sound of thunder can be very hyggeligt if you are inside and feel safe; if outside, not so much. SMELLS LIKE HYGGE Have you ever smelled something that takes you back to a time and place where you felt safe? Or smelled something that, more than a memory, gives you a flashback of how the world used to look when you were a child? Or maybe the smell of something provokes strong feelings of security and comfort, such as the aroma coming from a bakery, or the smell of apple trees in your childhood garden or maybe the familiar scent of your parents' house? What makes a smell hyggelig differs very much from person to person, because smells relate a situation to ones experienced with that smell in the past. For some people, the smell of cigarettes in the morning is the most hyggelig thing there is; to others, the smell may provoke nausea and headaches. One common element of all the smells of hygge is that they remind us of safety *and the sense of being cared for. We use smell to sense whether something is safe to eat, but we also use it to intuit whether a place is safe and how alert we should be. The smell of hygge is the smell that tells you to put your guard down completely. The smell of cooking, the smell of a blanket you use at home, or the smell of a place we perceive as safe can be very hyggeligt because it reminds us of a state of mind we experienced when we felt completely safe. WHAT DOES HYGGE FEEL LIKE? As I mentioned earlier, letting your fingers run across a wooden surface, around a warm ceramic cup, or through the hairs on the skin of a reindeer brings out the hygge. Old, homemade stuff that has taken a lot of time to make is always more hyggeligt than manufactured new stuff. And small things are always more hyggeligt than big things. If the slogan for the USA is "The bigger, the better," the slogan for Denmark is "The smaller, the more hyggeligt." In Copenhagen, almost all the buildings stand only three or four stories high. New houses made out of concrete, glass, and steel do not stand a chance against the hygge factor in these old buildings. Anything hand-crafted—objects created out of wood, ceramics, wool, leather, and so on—is hyggeligt. Shiny metal and glass are not hyggeligt—though they can be if they are old enough. The rustic, organic surface of something imperfect or something that has been or will be affected by age appeals to the touch of hygge. Also, the feeling of being inside something warm in a place where it is cold is very different from just being warm. It gives the feeling of being comfortable in a hostile environment. SEEING HYGGE Hygge is very much about light, as we have said. Too bright is not hyggeligt. But hygge is also very much about taking your time. This can be accentuated by watching very slow movements of things, for example, gently falling snow—or aqilokoq, as the Inuits would say—or the lazy flames from an open fire. In short, slow, organic movements and dark, natural colors are hyggelige. The sight of a bright, sterile hospital or watching fastmoving vehicles on a highway is not. Hygge is dimmed, rustic, and slow. THE SIXTH SENSE OF HYGGE Hygge is about feeling safe. Hence, hygge is an indication that you trust the ones you are with and where you are. And the feeling of hygge is an indication of your feeling of pleasure when someone tells you to go with your gut feeling, that you have expanded your comfort zone to include other people and feel you can be completely yourself around other people. So hygge can be tasted, heard, smelled, touched and seen. But, most important, hygge is felt. In the beginning of the book, I mentioned Winnie-the-Pooh, and I think his wisdom still holds true. You don't spell love. You feel it. This brings us to the final theme of the book: happiness.*

14

HYGGE (HAPPY LIVING) AND HAPPINESS

Today, political leaders from around the world are expressing an interest in why some societies are happier than others. At the same time, countries are taking steps to measure their success as a society—not only from how much the economy grows, but also from how much their lives are improved, not just by the standard of living but quality of life. This is one of the consequences of the paradigm shift away from gross domestic product (GDP) as the dominant indicator for progress in recent years. However, this idea is not new. As Robert Kennedy pointed out more than forty years ago: The gross national product does not allow for the health of our children, the quality of their education or the joy of their play. It does not include the beauty of our poetry or the strength of our marriages; the intelligence of our public debate or the integrity of our public officials . . . it measures everything, in short, except that which makes life worthwhile. Lately, this has increased the interest in and number of happiness surveys—and it seems that Denmark comes out on top almost every time. "About once a year, some new study confirms Denmark's status as a happiness superpower," wrote a journalist at The New York Times in 2009. Since then, the statement has become even truer. The World Happiness Report, which is commissioned by the United Nations, has now been published four times. Denmark has been in first place every time except once, when the country was pushed to third place. And the World Happiness Report is just one out of many rankings that puts Denmark and Copenhagen at the top of the lists about happiness and the country's livability. The same pattern is evident when the Organization for Economic Co-operation and Development looks at life satisfaction and when the European Social Survey looks at happiness. Monocle magazine has several times ranked Copenhagen as the world's most *livable city. Nowadays, well-being rankings are only news in Denmark when the country doesn't make first place. In addition, most Danes can't help but smile a little when they hear that Denmark is the happiest country in the world. They are well aware that Denmark was not first in line when weather was handed out and that when they are sitting in traffic on a wet February morning, they hardly look like the world's happiest people. So why are the people in Denmark so happy? THE HAPPY DANES As discussed, international surveys frequently name Denmark as the happiest country in the world, and this has naturally prompted an increasing interest on the part of happiness researchers. What are the reasons behind the high levels of happiness in Denmark? At the Happiness Research Institute, we have tried to answer this question in the report "The Happy Danes—Exploring the Reasons for the High Level of Happiness in Denmark." Briefly, there are many reasons. Several factors influence why some people and countries are happier than others:—genetics, our relationships, health, income, job, sense of purpose and freedom. But one of the main reasons why Denmark does so well in international happiness surveys is the welfare state, as it reduces uncertainty, worries, and stress in the population. You can say that Denmark is the happiest country in the world or you can say that Denmark is the least unhappy country in the world. The welfare state is really good (not perfect, but good) at reducing extreme unhappiness. Universal and free health care, free university education, and relatively generous unemployment benefits go a long way toward reducing unhappiness. This has particular significance for those who are less well off, a segment of society who is happier in Denmark than in other wealthy countries. Furthermore, there is a high level of trust in Denmark (notice all the strollers parked outside cafés when the parents are inside, drinking coffee). There is a high level of freedom (Danes report really high levels in terms of feeling in control over their lives), of wealth and good governance, and a well-functioning civil society. These factors, however, don't set Denmark apart from other Nordic countries. Norway, Sweden, Finland, and Iceland also enjoy relatively high levels of welfare. This is why all the Nordic countries are usually found in the top ten of happiness rankings. However, maybe the instance of hygge is what sets Denmark apart from the rest of the Nordic countries. I think hygge and happiness might be linked, as hygge may be the pursuit of everyday happiness and some of the key components of hygge are drivers of happiness. Let's look at some of them. HYGGE AS SOCIAL SUPPORT Given the above, we can now perhaps explain three-quarters of the reasons why some countries are happier than others—factors such as generosity, freedom, GDP, good governance, and healthy life expectancy. But the factor that has the biggest effect on our happiness is social support. What is meant by this is simply: do people have someone in their network they can rely on in times of need? Yes or no. It might not be the best or most nuanced way of measuring our social support systems, but it is the data we have across as many countries as are covered by the World Happiness Report. One of the reasons for the high level of happiness in Denmark is the good work– life balance, which allows people to make time for family and friends. According to the OECD Better Life Index, Danes have more free time than all the other OECD members, and according to the European Social Survey, 33 percent of Danes report feeling calm and peaceful all or most of the time, while the percentages are 23 for Germany, 15 in France, and 14 in the United Kingdom. So policies matter, but maybe hygge also fosters a special way of being together with your loved ones. In the chapter on togetherness, we touched on the link between relationships, hygge, and happiness. This link cannot be overstated. In 1943, the American psychologist Abraham Maslow developed a model called the pyramid of human needs and the theory that we must fill our needs from the bottom of the pyramid upward. The most elementary needs are physiological: food, water, and sleep—and security. But then come our social needs, our need for love and belonging. Without having these needs covered, we will not be able to move on to fulfilling our needs for self-esteem and self-actualization. Today, when happiness researchers analyze the common denominators among those who consider themselves happy, a pattern emerges without exception: happy people have meaningful and positive social relationships. Studies also show that when individuals experience social isolation, many of the same brain regions become active that are active in the experience of physical pain. The four editions of the World Happiness Report published thus far are packed with evidence of the link between relationships and happiness. Family and friends and close personal relationships with loved adults explain the greatest variation in happiness. Except in the very poorest countries, happiness varies more with the quality of our relationships than with wealth. According to the reports, the most important relationships are with loved ones— across all societies—but our relationships at work, with friends, and in the community are also important. So quality relationships impact our happiness, but the causality goes both ways. Studies suggest that having high levels of happiness leads to better social relationships. The reason may be that happiness increases our level of sociability and improves the quality of the relationships we have. Experiments also show that people in a positive mood express greater interest in social and pro-social activities. Similarly, according to the World Happiness Report, a world survey of 123 nations found that the experience of positive feelings was strongly related to good social relationships across different sociocultural regions. In sum, research from several decades provides evidence that supports the bond between our relationships and well-being. Happier people have a larger quantity and better quality of friendships and family relationships. Thus good relationships both cause happiness and are caused by it. The studies suggest that, of all the factors that influence happiness, a sense of feeling related to those around you is very near the top of the list. This is why hygge may be one of the reasons that Danes always report high levels of happiness. Not only are there policies that secure them time to pursue meaningful relationships, but the language and the culture also drive Danes to prioritize spending time with family and friends and to develop quality relationships over time. SAVORING AND GRATITUDE As mentioned in the chapter on food, hygge is about giving yourself and others a treat. It is about savoring the moment and the simple pleasures of good food and good company. It is giving the hot chocolate with whipped cream the attention it deserves. In short, indulgence. Hygge is about the now, how to enjoy the moment and make the best of it. More than anything, savoring is about gratitude. We often remind each other not to take things for granted. Gratitude is more than just a simple "thank you" when you receive a gift. It is about keeping in mind that you live right now, allowing yourself to focus on the moment and appreciate the life you lead, to focus on all that you do have, not what you don't. Clichés? Totally. Nevertheless, evidence-based studies show that practicing gratitude has an impact on happiness. According to Robert A. Emmons, a professor of psychology at University of California, Davis, and one of the world's leading experts on gratitude, people who feel grateful are not only happier than those who do not but also more helpful and forgiving and less materialistic. In one of his studies, which involved interviewing over a thousand people, some were told to keep gratitude journals, writing down what they were grateful for on a weekly basis. The researchers found that gratitude has psychological, physical, and social benefits. The people who wrote the gratitude journals reported feeling more positive emotions like alertness and enthusiasm, reported better sleep and fewer symptoms of disease, and were more mindful of situations where they could be helpful. Research also shows that grateful people tend to recover more quickly from trauma and suffering than others and are less likely to get stressed in different situations. You can see why it is important to include gratitude in your everyday life. Unfortunately, since our emotional system is a fan of newness, we are quick to adapt to new things and events, especially positive ones. Therefore, you need to come up with new things to be grateful for, and not get stuck in the same way of thinking. Emmons believes that gratitude makes people take a step back and see the value of what they have and thereby appreciate it more, which makes it less likely that they will take it for granted. Hygge may help us to be grateful for the everyday because it is all about savoring simple pleasures. Hygge is making the most of the moment, but hygge is also a way of planning for and preserving happiness. Danes plan for hyggelige times and reminisce about them afterward. "Is nostalgia part of hygge?" one of the designers of this book asked me. He had read some of the first drafts and we were now discussing the feel and visual identity at the Granola Café at Værnedamsvej in Copenhagen. At first I dismissed his idea. But in the process of writing, I slowly realized that he was right. Reliving hygge moments, sitting in front of the fire or on a balcony in the French Alps, or walking back into the summer cabin of my childhood, I was tripping on nostalgia. At the same time, I noticed that I was smiling. According to the study "Nostalgia: Content, Triggers, Function" in the Journal of Personality and Social Psychology (November 2006), nostalgia produces positive feelings, reinforces our memories and sense of being loved, and boosts self-esteem. So while happiness and hygge are definitely about appreciating the now, both may also be planned and preserved. Hygge and happiness have a past and a future as well as a present. HYGGE AS EVERYDAY HAPPINESS I study happiness. Each day, I try to answer one question: why are some people happier than others? I've been told that musicians can look at notes and hear the music in their heads. The same thing happens to me when I look at happiness data. I hear comforting sounds of lives well lived. I hear the joy, the feeling of connectedness, and the sense of purpose. Many people are, however, skeptical about the possibility of measuring happiness. One of the issues raised is that there are different perceptions of what happiness is. We try to acknowledge this by saying that "happiness" is an umbrella term. We break it down and look at the different components. So when the Happiness Research Institute, the UN, the OECD, and different governments try to measure happiness and quantify quality of life, we can consider at least three dimensions of happiness. First of all, we look at life satisfaction. We do this by asking people in international surveys: How satisfied are you with your life all in all? Or how happy are you on a scale from 0 to 10? Take a step back and evaluate your life. Think of the best possible life you could lead and the worst possible: Where do you feel you stand right now? This is where Denmark scores the highest in the world. Second, we look at the affective or hedonic dimension. What kind of emotions do people experience on an everyday basis? If you look at yesterday, did you feel angry, sad, lonely? Did you laugh? Did you feel happy? Did you feel loved? The third dimension is called the eudaemonic dimension. That is named after the ancient Greek word eudaimonia for "happiness." And it is based on Aristotle's perception of happiness. To him, the good life was a meaningful life.*

So do people experience a sense of purpose? Ideally, what we do is follow ten thousand or more people—in a scientific manner, not like a stalker—over, say, ten years. Because, over the next decade, some of us are going to get a promotion, some of us are going to lose our job, and some of us are going to get married. The question is: How do those changes in life circumstances impact the different dimensions of happiness? So how happy are you all in all? How satisfied are you with your life? These questions have been asked and answered millions of times across the world, so now we can look for patterns in the data. What do happy people have in common, whether you are from Denmark, the UK, the US, China, or India? What is the average effect on happiness from, say, doubling your income or getting married? What are the common denominators of happiness? We have been doing this for years when it comes to health, for example, looking into the common denominators of people who live to be a hundred years old. And because of those studies, we know that alcohol, tobacco, exercise, and our diet have an effect on our life expectancy. We use the same methods to understand what matters for happiness. So you might say, "Well, happiness is very subjective." Yes, of course it is, and it should be. What I care about is how you feel about your life. I think you are the best judge of whether you are happy or not. Yes, working with subjective measures is difficult, but it is not impossible. We do it all the time when it comes to stress, anxiety, and depression, which are also in some senses subjective phenomena. At the end of the day, it is all about how we as individuals perceive our lives. I have yet to hear a convincing argument why happiness should be the one thing in the world we cannot study in a scientific manner. Why should we not try to understand the thing that perhaps matters the most? So we try to understand what drives life satisfaction, affective or hedonic happiness, and eudaemonia. The different dimensions are linked, of course. If you have a day-to-day life that is filled with positive emotions, you are likely to report higher levels of life satisfaction. But the second dimension is much more volatile. We can detect a weekend effect here. People report more positive emotions during weekends than on weekdays. This would come as no surprise to most people, as we are more likely to engage in activities that bring out positive emotions during the weekend. Furthermore, the different dimensions of happiness are linked biologically. For instance, hedonic and eudaemonic well- being are correlated, and many of the brain mechanisms involved in the hedonic experience of sensory pleasure are also active in the more eudaemonic experience. Coming back to hygge and happiness, I think that one of the most interesting findings in recent years is that the experience of positive emotions matters more to our overall well-being, measured in terms of life satisfaction, than the absence of negative emotions (although both are important, according to the World Happiness Report). Researching and writing this book, I have come to realize that hygge may function as a driver for happiness on an everyday basis. Hygge gives us the language, the objective, and the methods for planning and preserving happiness —and for getting a little bit of it every day. Hygge may be the closest we come to happiness when we arrive home after a long day's work on a cold, rainy day in January. And let's face it, this is where most of our lives will play out. Not on cold, January days, but every day. Once a year—or more, if we are lucky—we may find ourselves on a beach in some exotic country and we may find both hygge and happiness on these distant shores. But hygge is about making the most of what we have in abundance: the everyday. Perhaps Benjamin Franklin said it best: "Happiness consists more in small conveniences or pleasures that occur every day, than in great pieces of good fortune that happen but seldom." Now, I am off to see my dad and his wife. I think I will take cake.

Getting to Know Your Brain

Your brain is built of cells called neurons and glia—hundreds of billions of them. Each one of these cells is as complicated as a city... Each cell sends electrical pulses to other cells, up to hundreds of times per second. If you represented each of these trillions and trillions of pulses in your brain by a single photon of light, the combined output would be blinding. The cells are connected to one another in a network of such staggering complexity that it bankrupts human language and necessitates new strains of mathematics... There are as many connections in a single cubic centimeter of brain tissue as there are stars in the Milky Way galaxy. —DAVID EAGLEMAN, INCOGNITO: THE SECRET LIVES OF THE BRAIN Getting to Know Your Brain 1 Your Brain: An Owner's Guide Inside your head is a three-pound marvel that rivals any technology in the world today. Sparked by the flow of electrical currents and an ever-changing blend of chemicals, each with a distinct job, it unendingly updates and remaps itself to make you possible. Powered by one hundred billion neurons, each connected to ten thousand additional neurons, the brain, many say, is the most complex object in the known universe. And what a job it does! It regulates your fundamental body functions: your breath, heart rate, and digestion. It regulates sleep, hunger, growth, and hormonal cycles. It processes memories. Emotions. Cravings, and how you indulge them. It manages how you sense and navigate the world. All this, and an unending list beyond, is the work of your brain, often without you even knowing what it's up to. Your brain also does things you're very much aware of. It lets you carefully place a bandage on a child's knee, mindfully directing muscle movements that otherwise simply happen. It guides how you close your eyes and inhale slowly when you smell something delicious, savoring the aromas— and the moment. When you organize how you'll study for a test, consider why you should (or shouldn't) get a puppy, carefully explain a process to a new employee, or stop yourself from losing your temper, you guessed it: you're also using your brain.But you're using different brain functions, and even different brain areas, for the various actions just described. Our brains are so complex it's hard to explain them in any one description. They remain mysterious, even with ever-advancing work in neuroscience and other cognitive sciences: linguistics, psychology, anthropology, artificial intelligence, philosophy, and more. Textbooks, websites, even popular shows explore the brain's intricacies. Yet no one discipline seems to give us a full understanding of how our brains really work—or how we can work with them. To begin to understand the brain, we could take an anatomical approach, reviewing the brain's specific regions and each of their unique roles. We could explore the chemistry of the brain, discussing how neurotransmitters and hormones modulate brain activity. We could look to psychology, studies of consciousness, or other disciplines seeking to understand life through the perspective of the brain. All of these ways are fascinating. No one path, though, does the whole job. To paint a full picture, this book borrows from a range of disciplines—neuroscience, psychology, spirituality, anthropology, and more. It shares wisdom from great thinkers, from respected leaders, and from a range of artists and innovators who've left meaningful marks on the world. We'll look at all of this through the lens of happiness, sharing enough about the brain to ignite new ways of thinking about it as you make decisions about your life—and your path to satisfaction. The Happiness Hack 4 The point of this book is to give you a glimpse of what's going on inside your head so you can work with your brain's tendencies and potential in new ways. Your brain, after all, is something of a "prediction machine," working nonstop to keep you safe and alive.

It constantly updates itself with incoming information from the world around you and integrates those updates to the vast stores of information collected across your entire life experience. When new information comes in, the brain calls on existing, dependable pathways, or maps, to guide its response. Left to itself, it will stick, often stubbornly, to those well-worn pathways—even if they're not leading us in the desired direction. That can make change hard. It's almost as if the brain is saying, "If it's worked so far, keep doing it. If it's new, it's risky—so resist." "Worked," to the brain, is pretty simple. For the brain, if you're here, you've survived, so what you've done in the past must be working. Regardless of how happy your past decisions, outlooks, or actions have made you, to the brain, it's been a winning strategy. But, as this book will explain, you can often have a say in which pathways the brain uses, or even paves: the old familiar go-tos or new ones you choose. What's more, as you choose new ways, moving from automatic decisions to intentional ones, your brain will continue to update its pathways. With time, those pathways will become part of your brain's map of "what works," helping those once-new actions become easy, even automatic, routines. To start understanding this, let's look at some brain basics.

Your Brain = The Digital World One zettabyte of information: it even sounds like a lot. And it is. In fact, it's so big, we have to describe it in ways most of us have never imagined before. Haven't heard of a zettabyte? You're not alone: it's a term recently coined to describe the amount of digital information stored in the world today But that's how much information it would take to plot a threedimensional map of just one brain's wiring. According to Princeton computational neuroscientist Sebastian Seung, who creates "slice images" human brains to map the way neurons connect in the brain, it would take a full zettabyte of information— the equivalent of all digital information in the world— to reveal the wiring between all of the connections.1 A byte, you may know, is a unit of digital information. A letter, number, or character generally takes up one byte of computer memory. A zettabyte is 1,000,000,000,000,000,000,000 bytes. For reference, it would take seventy-five billion sixteen- gigabyte iPads to store a zettabyte of information. Your brain may weigh only three pounds, but it truly is among the most complicated objects in the world.

We can cluster the brain's functions into three basic categories. MANAGING OUR BODIES: THE HINDBRAIN The brain, obviously, largely controls the body. It directs operations we're not always aware of (like heart or breathing rate) or don't know how to be aware of (try activating your spleen to see for yourself). It regulates appetite and sleep cycles, and guides our biological desires to eat or sleep. It also coordinates digestive processes, balance, and hormone levels. These functions and countless others integrate across many different parts of the brain. However, generally speaking, the bodyoriented parts of our brains span the regions stacked on the spinal column from the back of our necks to the center of the brain. The body management parts of the brain are the most ancient and the ones most similar to other animals' brains. Their functions are highly efficient and largely invisible to us: we are neither conscious of nor in control of most of their work. As we move up and toward the forehead, the brain areas become more distinctly human, and less autonomous, in their processing.

HOUSING MEMORIES AND EMOTIONS: THE LIMBIC SYSTEM Feelings and memories are essential tools for navigating human life. They're so important the brain manages them in a dedicated center: the limbic system, a fist-sized region nestled around the central core of the brain. The limbic system's location hints at how integrated it is with both body and cognitive processes. Humans are social animals. Our ability to interact with others, and to use feelings to guide our actions, helped early humans survive. Memories, sensitivities, and responses—personal perspectives inform our relationship to the world around us, even without our awareness. We may not realize it, but our memories and emotions guide the way we make sense of, and take action in, our moment-to-moment experiences.

Have you ever made a rubber band ball? You take the rubber bands found wrapped around newspapers, bunches of carrots, or holding your shoeboxes closed—maybe even one the schoolyard bully shot at you from across the playground—and wrap them around each other, building outward. Maybe you started with a pebble in the center. Maybe a little wad of paper. Or maybe just a first rubber band. And you keep building, for weeks, months, even years. After a while, you may not recall what's at the center of the ball. But it's still there, affecting every layer wrapped around it. So it goes with memories and emotions. Some are on the surface, visible to you and easy to identify. Some are hidden a bit beneath, not entirely visible or identifiable—but as important to the way you (and your brain!) navigate your experiences as they are to the structure of that rubber band ball. Psychologically speaking, that's kind of how the brain builds memories and emotions. We layer new perceptions upon old ones, even upon old ones we can't see. Knowing what's on the outside is one thing; often, we're aware of the newer stuff. It's the older stuff that tends to go invisible. Yet we build our new memories and emotions upon them. Even when we don't sense or remember what's hidden inside, they're there. PROCESSING INFORMATION AND THOUGHT: THE CORTEX The brain processes massive amounts of information from emotions, the senses, prior learning, and much more as it directs what to do next. This is the work of the cortex, that lumpy outer covering we often think of when we visualize the brain. Although common images of the brain tend to show it as a continuous assembly of wrinkly tissue, the cortex is actually made up of numerous domains, each with specific functions. Sensory information from the outside world, language, perception, thought, and more are all processed here. Most of this processing— as much as 90 percent, according to some theories— happens without our awareness. The brain takes everything it's mapped so far and calculates, in an instant, how to react. Only a fraction of our thinking is actually intentional in the "thoughtful and aware" sense. Why? Well, the brain is made to act fast. After all, speedy decisions— ones we don't even have to "think" about— have saved our ancestral bacon since the dawn of time.

Yet some of our brains' fast decisions may not be the ones we'd choose if we had, or took, time to think about them. With due respect to the brain's ability to act fast, there are times when the speedy reaction isn't the best. Think about the moments when you've snapped at a friend, blurted out the wrong answer, or chomped down that extra slice of pizza and you'll sense how unintentional the brain's fast decisions can be. Fast thinking— often the repetition of actions you've habitually taken or thoughts you've had before— is the brain's default mode. But it doesn't always lead to our most satisfying outcomes.

For those, we need to shift gears, and that takes awareness and effort. Intentional or mindful thinking is slower, less efficient, and less habitual than the brain's usual routines. Yet this sort of thinking often leads to more satisfying long- term results than routine reactions deliver. Generally speaking, intentional processing happens in the most recently evolved part of the human cortex: most of the brain's real estate is dedicated to this information-processing capacity. What we generally see in a picture of the brain—that gray, wrinkly, bicycle helmet–shaped stuff? That's where information perception and processing happens. This area, generally called the cortex, occupies about 75 percent of the brain's mass. In the cortex, you'll find everything you need to sense and make sense out of the outside world, along with the areas you call on when things don't make sense. In other words, it's where you receive, integrate, process, and decide how to act on information in both fast (default) and slow (intentional) ways. the pfc brain: the prefrontal cortex, or PFC. The PFC occupies the area behind your forehead. Rest your palms at your temples, fingers pointing in, and you'll pretty much cover its territory. The PFC is the home of complex cognition including planning, critical thought, and impulse control. It's where we make conscious decisions and evaluate trade-offs, and where we find ways to resist the easy actions and choose the ones we really want. These types of thinking are often referred to as "higher cognitive functions." They're the willful thoughts we hold in our minds and reflect on when we mindfully direct decisions rather than let the brain's automatic processes decide for us. Although we can roughly describe the functions of the brain within these three contexts—body management, emotional and memory processing, and interpreting information and thought, it's not quite that simple. The brain is a complex, cohesive system. It integrates information from multiple areas to perform even relatively simple processes. This three-part framework paints a general picture of what the brain does, and where it does it, so you can apply that understanding in the chapters ahead. Mindfulness "Mindful" is a word often applied to willful or intentional thinking: that "held in mind" thought we direct to the prefrontal cortex. We can think of mindfulness as the act of interrupting the brain's tendency toward routine, reactive, and fast processing. Instead, we shift, intentionally, to aware, directed thinking. Consider the basic brain areas and their functions: managing bodily functions, housing memory and emotion, and processing information. All three of these modes work together and simultaneously. We can flow, shift, or even be jolted from one mode to another. For the most part, our body functions are invisible to us: completely autonomous. Normally, for example, we don't think about breathing. But we can. We can control our breathing rate, or hold our breath. We can learn to breathe differently (think swimming or meditation) to the point where it becomes unconscious or even automatic to breathe that way. But most of the time, breathing, like other bodily functions, happens at a level that we don't, and even can't, control. Memory, emotion, perception, and thought are different. Although generally these levels of processing are unconscious, we have a different level of agency with them than we do, say, with the way we breathe while we're asleep. We can, for example, work our way back to memories or feelings and gain insight into how they affected us. We can practice managing our emotions, finding new ways to process things like anger, sadness, negativity, or fear. We can train our perceptions, learning to tune out background noise, overcome a fear of heights, or enjoy spicy foods. We can also learn to be aware of our thoughts (some of them, at least), shifting them to where we can control them rather than letting them mindlessly control us. A fun way to think about this is by imagining two cars. One is an engineering marvel: a full-featured, fast, automated beauty loaded with bells and whistles. Generally speaking, it runs in driverless mode, managing speed, monitoring traffic, optimizing your route, and alerting you when it needs something. But you don't really have to think about it. You're simply along for the ride. Now, sometimes you'd override that car if you wanted to. If a scenic vista caught your eye as you cruised down the highway, you could flip the turn signal and pull over to take in the view.

But unless you took action, that car would keep rolling on. It wouldn't be concerned with helping you enjoy the scenery. It would work to get you where you're going, on time— and to keep you safe as you got there. Then, imagine another car: a slow moving off- road vehicle that guzzled gas, needed regular maintenance, and took work to get started— but got you to places you couldn't reach any other way. If you could, you'd flip between these cars for different drives. You'd slide into the driverless car for everyday commutes, letting it do the work so you could relax while it navigated the road.

Sometimes you'd override it, challenging the preprogrammed agenda and taking a different route than it suggested, then letting it take over again. Yet for some drives, you'd fire up that off- road buggy and put your hands on the wheel, pointing it exactly where you wanted to go. You'd feel confident it was up to the job, despite the work it took to drive. You'd know it had the features and functions to get you places that sleek cruiser could never go. But you might check the oil first. Here's some good news: both of those vehicles are parked in your cranial garage. There's even better news. These two vehicles tend to travel together, ready for you to shift— or be shifted— between them, depending on your needs. Normally, the driverless car would own the road, cruising along without needing a thing from you. Now and again it might come across a bumpy passage, or a place without an available map. Then it would shift things over to the off- road vehicle, shifting back once the tricky part had been navigated.

Generally speaking, a driverless car doesn't really need a driver. The person in the driver's seat is actually more of a passenger. Sometimes, though, a driver wants something different from its car's preprogrammed plan, familiar and efficient as that it may be. There's scenery to notice. A path less followed that's about something more than getting there fast. Or simply the skill and enjoyment of driving a hands-on car, and getting better at it with practice. So it goes with our brains. Most of the time, they're driverless: automatically following the programmed routes. The thing is, the routes they've learned and optimized may not be the ones the driver wants to keep traveling. Sometimes we want to take back the wheel and head in a different direction, tricky as the gears might feel at first. This kind of driving puts the skill, and the work, into the hands of the driver. Try It Out Take a cookie break while you think about this, even if it's only with an imaginary cookie. Grab one, fast, and chomp into it. By the time the cookie is gone, you'll barely even know you've eaten it. Next, take a nice little bite, maybe while you look out your window at the view outside. Pay attention to the scenery and the taste of the cookie. Sip some coffee and savor the contrast in flavors. Then, slow down and take an even smaller bite, examining the texture on your teeth and layers of subtle flavors melting on your tongue.

That's what it's like to shift gears, exploring the range of awareness we can bring to an experience—and sensing the transitions between brain modalities. Who Runs the Show? The brain runs the show, right? Isn't that what it's for? Well, if you're in that driverless car, then yes: the brain is in charge. Managing your body and processing some 90 percent of thoughts and actions? Thank goodness we're in a state-of-the-art cruiser for that amount of work. After all, the brain is a hungry organ. Although it occupies only 2 percent of our adult body mass, it consumes some 20 percent of our energy supply. It runs on glucose (metabolized sugar) and oxygen, and it's ravenous for both. Take either away, even for a moment, and the brain slows down. Go longer, and there's actual danger. Drops in glucose correlate with problems in thinking, memory, and impulse control. Lack of oxygen? We know those dangers. Four to six minutes without oxygen and the brain suffers irreversible damage—or even death. By operating efficiently, the brain conserves glucose and oxygen, keeping it available for whatever might be coming around the bend. So it operates in automatic mode whenever it can. In other words, it runs the show. But if you're shifting to that other car, something else seems to take over. That thing seems to take charge, at least when it can get behind the wheel. Mindfulness activates that thing, whatever it is. It takes some of the control away from the programmed processes and puts it in the The mind controls the brain controls the mind. —DAVID ROCK, AUTHOR, FOUNDER OF THE NEUROLEADERSHIP INSTITUTE

hands of a "driver": one with an intention or agenda that can differ from what the automatic car would choose. Many religious, spiritual, and psychological traditions talk about this driving force. Some call it the mind. Some may say the spirit, or the soul; some the superego. Others assert that the force is simply another brain function. These differing voices can agree to only one thing: that no one really knows. And we don't have to know. Yet one practice, Buddhism, offers a friendly term to describe this force: the Watcher. This is a simple reference to "whatever it is" that watches our thoughts and actions, but is separate from those thoughts and actions. Like the passenger or driver of those cars, sometimes it's active and sometimes it's not. Sometimes it's along for the ride and sometimes it owns the road. In either mode, it can be watchful, and aware. Passively or actively, the Watcher is mindful. Putting the Watcher on Watch The Watcher sounds useful, right? Something that directs us to awareness, guides big-picture thinking, and coaches us to say, "But, on the other hand..." It is useful. We all have examples of times when we did our best work by resisting the easy, default approach (like that automatic car's programmed route) and thought through a better way. We feel good about those moments and less so about the times when we acted fast, reacted automatically, and regretted the consequences later. But the Watcher can't be on duty full-time. Think of the Watcher as a highly paid worker. "Watcher" thinking activates the brain's newest and often less efficient area: that "off- road" prefrontal cortex, or PFC. Of all of the brain's parts, the PFC is the least fuel- efficient. Which gives us a clue to why the brain tends to stay in that automatic mode. Science is still cracking the code on precisely how much extra juice the PFC demands, but we get a hint when we look at energy consumed by the brains of other primates. Whereas our furrier relatives tend to use around 10 percent of their energy to fuel their brains, we humans— the ones with the big PFCs— seem to use around twice that. The PFC gets tired fast. If you've ever gone blank while solving a complicated problem, had your temper flare pointlessly when you were tired, or thought "My brain hurts" after an intense planning session, you've felt that depletion. After all, in the world we evolved for, we needed our energy for things other than orchestrating long- term projects, staying sharp during a long day at the office, or navigating a world of constantly buzzing distractions. Mostly, we worked on surviving, and surviving meant saving energy. The brain's first job was to keep us alive. Being prepared to fight with or run from whatever was lurking around the corner (or rustling in the grass) meant conserving energy. If a task wasn't geared for survival, our brains made sure there was some resistance to doing it.

Today, we often face decisions served better by thoughtful reflection than by lightning-fast reactions. Yet the resistance ingrained in our brains has not gone away. However, if we're looking to bring more happiness into our lives, to align with purpose, or to feel more mastery and self-control, we need a different path. It involves the Watcher as well as an understanding of how today's reality can scramble our signals and leave us feeling less than happy—or in charge. Understanding that means looking at what happiness actually is. It also means thinking about the things that lead to real happiness, the kind we all hunger for. Finding those things may mean disconnecting from some things we've assumed or simply done because they've become automatic habits. We've defaulted to them and forgotten to be watchful. Routing our path to happiness means learning how, and when, to put our hands back on that metaphorical wheel. It means looking at routes that have become so familiar our automatic mode thinks they are the way, not merely a way. And it means investing the energy, and the practice, in activating parts of our brains that can fall out of use when we get too swept up in automatic mode— the brain's most powerful and efficient way of working. It's easy to fall into automatic mode. We all do it. Yet learning to take back some control turns out to be a path to more happinessand satisfaction than we can find in the habitual paths. Even the work of taking the wheel, it turns out, helps us enjoy the road. And the practice of doing that helps boost the brain's capacity to do more of it. This is mindful work, the work of the Watcher—and something anyone can learn. There are many ways to start activating this practice. One proven route hinges on something so basic to human nature that we often take it for granted or forget to actively nurture it. Especially in these busy, often distracting times, it's a time-honored benefit that often slips by the wayside. It's a simple thing, yet so core to our well-being and satisfaction that it's worth working to reclaim. It happens when we build connections. Chemistry More than a hundred unique chemicals flow through your brain at any given time. Their levels and activity are regulated by a range of factors: everything from your genetics to what's happening in your environment to how you've lived your life so far. Here, meet some of the most common and well-understood brain chemicals—both neurotransmitters and hormones—affecting happiness, health, and social interactions.

Dopamine: Ah, the thrill of the chase...the pursuit of a worthy goal...even the ping of an incoming "Like"! Meet dopamine: sparking feelings of enjoyment and gratification (as well as indulgence in guilty pleasures). This neurotransmitter boosts our happiness when we pursue or reach a goal...but can draw us in to too much of a good (or bad) thing. Serotonin: There's nothing like the view from the *top! Fulfillment, alignment with purpose, pride of long-term accomplishments: serotonin is the neurotransmitter often associated with selfesteem and life satisfaction. It helps you appreciate, enjoy, and reflect positively on the moments and achievements that have shaped the journey.*

Endorphins: You can do it! Endorphins kick in when we're exercising, helping us power through resistance...or even pain. The runner's high, the athletic rush: they're what we get when these hormones are on the job. Good news: they also show up when we're laughing, and all-around help us feel more pleasure and less pain. Cortisol: Although normal levels help regulate our bodies, watch out: this hormone can build up with long-term stress and affect mental and physical health. Cortisol levels rise over time when we're chronically exposed to negative or threatening situations. Good news: healthy diet, exercise, rest, and mindfulness practices can all help to reduce cortisol levels.

Adrenaline: Defend your turf or run like the wind! Excitement, arousal, danger: this hormone gets us up and moving...fast. Stressful situations fire it up as it prepares us for fight-or-flight. Adrenaline, also called epinephrine, shifts us into high gear in situations that are threatening, stressful, and/or physically exhilarating.

Bonding, caring, affection, connection: our "cuddle hormones" draw and keep us together. In women, oxytocin takes the lead in making the magic happen. For men, it's vasopressin. Either way, they help us feel the love...and keep the closeness coming. Aside from feeling nice, these hormones act as part of the glue of human connection. They help attract, draw, and keep us together

Bonding, caring, affection, connection: our "cuddle hormones" draw and keep us together. In women, oxytocin takes the lead in making the magic happen. For men, it's vasopressin. Either way, they help us feel the love...and keep the closeness coming. Aside from feeling nice, these hormones act as part of the glue of human connection. They help attract, draw, and keep us together

The Greeks puzzled over happiness for generations. Happiness, according to the philosopher Aristippus (c. 435–256 BCE), was pleasure—and as much of it as possible. Indulgence was the goal. Values, to him, had no real worth. Aristippus's beliefs inspired the term "hedonic happiness," a label often given to impulsive and indulgent pleasures or the temporary relief of urges. In contrast, "eudaimonic happiness," taught by Aristotle (384– 322 BCE), elicited a deep well-being found in aligning with purpose, conquering obstacles, and achieving growth. This happiness grew from a virtuous life and the quest to actualize our potential. Tequila shots or video games wouldn't have made Aristotle's cut (if they'd been around in ancient Greece). Guilty pleasures and easy indulgences were not on the eudaimonic menu. Aristippus and Aristotle may have lived before the dawn of cognitive neuroscience, but their thinking pointed to something we now know is true. Different feelings of happiness correlate to the presence of distinctly different brain chemicals. Hedonic pleasures, generally, are the domain of dopamine: the chemical frequently associated with the chase of a desired object. Indulging urges, being distracted, or having "just one more" are generally dopamine-spiked behaviors that don't usually lead to lasting satisfaction. Eudaimonic rewards, on the other hand, are linked to a different chemical: serotonin, which increases feelings of worthiness, belonging, and self-esteem. "To increase serotonin," says endurance athlete and author Christopher Bergland, "challenge

yourself regularly and pursue things that reinforce purpose, meaning, and accomplishment. Being able to say 'I did it!' produces a feedback loop that reinforces confidence and creates an upward spiral of serotonin." Both dopamine and serotonin help us feel pleasure and happiness. Yet for all of the good dopamine does—motivating us, helping us learn, literally getting us up and moving—it can wreak havoc on blood pressure, cause nervous tics, and elevate anxiety. It's associated with compulsive or addictive behaviors and can drive distraction, impulsivity, and lack of self-control. Serotonin is different. Generally speaking, the body doesn't naturally produce too much of it. Having too little is a bigger issue: low levels of serotonin are associated with lethargy, binge eating, mood swings, and depression. So earning healthier happiness by choosing Aristotle's way over Aristippus's is good for your body as well as your brain. Now, brain chemicals aren't bad or good. They're all necessary, and they each contribute to keeping our minds and bodies functioning. But many casinos, advertisers, politicians, and even technology designers understand, or at least intuit, how these chemicals work—and use them to their advantage. Often, there's a deliberate plan to hook you on what they offer and keep you wanting more. Even without intent, anyone with an agenda can exploit the *dark side of dopamine's power by activating your desires and promising you satisfaction through what they offer. There's a big difference between the satisfaction Aristotle*

encouraged and the indulgence Aristippus sought. Though they pondered happiness long ago, the questions they asked then remain at least as relevant today. What is the happiness we seek? What causes it, and why do we long for it? Above all, what are we willing to do to build that happiness? And are we sure the happiness we're seeking is actually real satisfaction, rather than the easy tumble into distraction and indulgence dangled before us at every turn in the modern world?

Building Connections

L ooking at the technology and data, you might assume we all feel more connected to each other than ever. After all, billions of us log in to Facebook every day. We search Google 2.5 billion times and send more than 6 billion text messages every twenty-four hours. And the count is rising. On Snapchat, we share 9,000 snaps per second. Yet other data—about people, not technology—tells a different story. One out of four Americans reports struggling with loneliness. One in five finds it persistent. Depression is on the rise as a global health risk, predicted to be the world's second most prevalent medical condition (heart disease is number one) by 2020. And depression, research shows, is often a disease of loneliness. We may be connected, technically speaking. But our digital connections don't necessarily leave us feeling that way. In fact, they might be making us feel more alone. And feeling connected, with real people, is at the very core of our ability to be happy. Interaction vs. Transaction Access to technology has brought us all kinds of efficiencies that make life easier, smoother, and more predictable. We rely on our tech to help us do more faster and to automate an increasing number of everyday processes. Efficiencies are great. But they're not why we're here. Our lives mean more than simply saving time so we can get more done. Satisfaction doesn't grow from doing more stuff, some of it meaningless, faster and faster. And all that time we spend staring at screens—half of our waking hours for the average American—is time we don't spend on things that can make us happier. Screens don't lead us to happiness. Our brains know it, and our hearts feel it. Stress levels climb, year over year, yet nobody knows how to break the cycle. Our bodies know it too. Loneliness hurts, and that's more than a metaphor. UCLA psychologist Naomi Eisenberger studied how feelings of loneliness and exclusion triggered activity in some of the brain regions associated with senses of physical pain. Social pain, her research showed, could hurt so much people physically felt it. We're here to interact, not simply to transact. On some level, we seem to know this. But distractions from tech and other temptations promise easy answers and quick fixes only a click away, so we keep clicking. Happiness for an hour: take a nap. Happiness for a day: go fishing. Happiness for a year: inherit a fortune. Happiness for a lifetime? Help someone else. —CHINESE PROVERB Messages all around us try to convince us that happiness is simply one more purchase, night on the town, or date away. Even as FOMO (fear of missing out) rivets us to our devices, calling us to document rather than enjoy the moment (in hopes of winning flurries of "likes"), many of us feel more and more alone. The very action of capturing and sharing our moments directs us toward our tech and away from the only lasting source of happiness: the real world and the people around us. Not convinced? Multiple studies show that when we snap a quick picture, we barely retain the memory of what the camera saw. The brain seems to decide we've outsourced that memory, so it doesn't bother to map it. We capture it. Yet we don't retain it. Social platforms put us in the shallows, so to speak, of interaction. A quick "like" or "sad face" may signal engagement to the person on the other side of the post and release a quick chemical that may feel like happiness, but it's fleeting. Our retention of what we liked or were sad about on social platforms doesn't last. Nor does it really connect us to people. We've all seen posts on social media about friends' losses or heartbreaks. Yet we may not recall the loss when we encounter that friend in real life. As we tune in to our tech instead of to each other, we pay a price.

It is not the forces of darkness but of shallowness that everywhere threaten the true, and the good, and the beautiful, and that ironically address themselves as deep and profound. It is an exuberant and fearless shallowness that everywhere is the modern danger, and that everywhere nonetheless calls to us as savior.
—KEN WILBUR, PSYCHOLOGIST, SCHOLAR, AUTHOR

Connecting IRL Connecting IRL (in real life) is no longer the simple, natural action it once was. Even in the real world, we disconnect. Scan the line at your favorite coffee shop and see how many people are looking at their phones, not at each other. How many stay glued to them even as they place their order and leave the counter without saying "hello" or "thank you" to the person who took their order? We may think this doesn't matter: that small, casual interactions don't register in the brain as connection. But they do. A smile activates mirror neurons— special signals that fire when we act and when we observe others acting— making grins literally contagious. Smiles are like parties for the brain. They activate neuropeptides that work to reduce stress and spread happy messages throughout the body. Dopamine, serotonin, and endorphins also fire up, triggering relaxation and lowering blood pressure. Sensations of pain may ease, thanks to endorphins. Both the smiler and the "smilee" usually feel a mood boost. We shall never know all the good a simple smile can do.

We shall never know all the good a simple smile can do. —MOTHER TERESA

Friendly eye contact works even better. Human eyes are unique: our pupils are surrounded by white, and the shape of our eye opening makes sure the white is visible. Why? Anthropologists propose that our more-open eyes helped us know who to trust and cooperate with. Most primate babies watch the head direction of the grown-up primates they're learning from. But human babies do something different: they watch eyes. In fact, a Purdue University study found that eye contact, even short glances between strangers, sparked a feeling of connection that wasn't experienced when subjects looked the other way. In their research, people who didn't receive eye contact, even in casual settings, reported feeling ignored and unseen, a feeling that hurt. The only reason we don't open our hearts and minds to other people is that they trigger confusion in us that we don't feel brave enough or sane enough to deal with. To the degree that we look clearly and compassionately at ourselves, we feel confident and fearless about looking into someone else's eyes. —PEMA CHÖDRÖN, BUDDHIST NUN, AUTHOR

Think about that chain reaction as you look to that coffee shop line. Connection as a Survival Mechanism Neuroscientist and social psychologist John Cacioppo has dedicated his career to understanding loneliness and its effect on the brain and body. "The absence of social connection triggers the same primal alarm bells as hunger, thirst, and physical pain," he explains. "Loneliness puts your brain into self-preservation mode... The visual cortex becomes more active while the area responsible for empathy becomes less active." In self-preservation mode, higher-level thinking becomes more elusive. We lock into default patterns, making it harder to access the Watcher or the functions of the PFC. The brain handles social threat and physical threat in similar ways, firing the fight-orflight response, which reduces blood supply to the PFC and even, through the adrenal system, to our vital organs.

There is a word in South Africa—Ubuntu—a word that captures Mandela's greatest gift: his recognition that we are all bound together in ways that are invisible to the eye; that there is a oneness to humanity; that we achieve ourselves by sharing ourselves with others, and caring for those around us. —PRESIDENT BARACK OBAMA, SPEAKING AT THE MEMORIAL SERVICE

We feel it. When we feel shunned in a social setting, our caution grows. The brain locks in to subconscious or unconscious patterns, searching for what has worked before. Maybe we reach for another drink or chomp a bite of something we don't really want. We feel diminished, even confused. As we grab the drink and grease-burger and head for the more predictable reward system of our apps, email, or TV, we pay a price. Dr. Cacioppo's work shows that loneliness is even riskier than obesity in some age groups. Social isolation is correlated to a 20 percent increase in mortality rates relative to "not lonely" research groups. As we continue to direct our attention to things rather than to people, our brains adapt and rewire, making this shift the new normal. But this normal isn't leading us to happiness. It can leave us feeling lost, out of sorts, and alone. Timeless Wisdom "I see you" is a traditional greeting used in some southern African cultures. Sometimes another phrase, "I am here to be seen," completes the greeting, creating a circle of acknowledgment. You can almost feel the mirror neurons firing. These respectful, socially connecting words likely rose into custom as a declaration of good intent. But they signal something core to human happiness: our need to connect with each other. "I see you" hints at the African concept of Ubuntu, which tells us that "A person is a person through other people." Our brains would agree.

How often do we feel ignored? How many people do we pass each day whom we never notice or acknowledge? How many more if we're tuned to our cell phones? Do we really "see" others when we tap "like" on a social post? When digital transactions serve as proxy for real-life interactions, we feel invisible and excluded. A deeper sort of FOMO can kick in. Fortunately, there's another path, one that helps fire our brain's reward chemicals and wire new maps to happier patterns. Neuroplasticity—the brain's ability to update itself by mapping new neural connections—gives us the power to reclaim pathways we've unintentionally lost and build new ones. But we have to get out of automatic mode. It takes intention—and practice. Yet as the brain fires, so it wires. Which gives you a good reason to start doing more of whatever it is you really want to do, especially if that means reconnecting with people. Here are some ways to get started. Disconnect to Reconnect If feeling more connected sounds good to you, try these simple steps. LOOK UP FROM THE TECH Choose one real-world thing

you'd like to do more of and one screen-based thing you'd like to do less of. Jot your intentions down, and put them somewhere visible, where you see them every day. Celebrate your progress, and start again if you lapse. Building or breaking habits takes work. But learning, it turns out, activates parts of your brain that contribute to feelings of wellbeing and mastery. What's more, integration of new information or actions often take place in the PFC, revving up parts of the brain that help us build willpower, make satisfying decisions, and mindfully navigate what's going on around us. The best place to meet people? Easy: anywhere your TV is not. START SMALL The brain maps familiar thoughts and actions with ever-increasing efficiency. For better or worse, these maps make it easy to see and do things the way we have in the past. We become blind to these assumptions: they become automatic. Changing them takes work and repetition. So even small changes can start out slowly. To reduce resistance, work with your brain. Associate new patterns with familiar actions. This helps your brain build new actions on existing maps. Slip your phone into your pocket as you walk toward the coffee shop. Remind yourself to say good morning before you place your order. Watch what happens. Want positive reinforcement? Try smiling. As your mirror neurons fire when that barista smiles back, your brain will update its maps and prime itself for smiling more, with increasingly less effort. Smile...it makes people wonder what you're up to.
—UNKNOWN

VOLUNTEER Every community, every destination, every affinity group likely needs more help than they are getting. What do you believe in? Who or what do you want to support? Getting hands-on with something that makes a difference is a surefire way to experience a brain-nourishing (and heart-filling) form of satisfaction. And it's a great way to connect with others. You're likely to find kindred spirits—and the deep satisfaction of contributing toward a shared goal. Be a rainbow in someone else's cloud. —MAYA ANGELOU, AUTHOR AND PRESIDENTIAL INAUGURAL POET rainbow RETHINK SOLITUDE "Loneliness," said theologian Paul Tillich, "expresses the pain of being alone, and solitude expresses the glory." Sometimes what seems to be loneliness can actually be a sense of disconnection from purpose. Yes, we all need and deserve social connection. But we also desire and deserve a feeling that we're making a difference in the world: that our contributions matter.

You matter. As do your contributions, whatever they may be. Yet our sense of purpose can get sucked into the vortex of everyday reality, with its unending to-do lists, commutes, and pressures. We come home feeling worn and depleted. Understandably, we crave the low-resistance stuff. But too much vegging out can eat into happiness. The typical triggers and rewards of apps or video games, TV series, or even our inboxes activate brain chemicals that can increase our sense of stress, isolation, and threat. When we feel those, we're less open to social engagement. We shut down and stay in, which weakens the maps that show us how to open back up again. How can we reverse the cycle and turn alone time into satisfying time? Self-care is one place to begin. Even small things that take care of you are a surefire way to find strength in solitude. Cooking well for yourself, even once a week, or perfecting a yoga sun salutation...each small step can help you and your body find a bit of glory. Since the brain wires what it fires, you'll also get a boost that helps point you toward the next healthy step. Since we know dopamine cues motivation and progress toward rewards, we can use that knowledge to boost our healthy drives. If your homeward commute is usually filled with dreams of vegging out, visualize yourself drawing in your sketchbook or practicing that new guitar chord instead. Invite the Watcher to help, helping your brain prime itself for your desired activity. Not convinced? Consider this: competitive athletes use similar brain exercises as they train and prepare to compete. If it's good enough for them, you deserve it too.

BE PATIENT Somewhere inside, we know connections are key to happiness. In a way, feelings of loneliness or isolation are like a signal telling us we want something other than what we have. Yet, ironically, feelings of loneliness can actually make us more self-protective. When we feel threatened, it's true: we tend to shut down. That's how our brains work, for all sorts of complicated reasons. Yet we're conditioned to blame ourselves, to think it's a problem with us. Sadly, the more we think this, the more our responses can lock the loneliness in. Sometimes even our best attempts don't go as we planned. We may be friendlier in the outside world or make efforts to mingle with new people, but the "tribe finding" doesn't go as we'd hoped. That can be hard. But try to remember that everyone's experiencing the stress and distraction of everyday life. Even with the help of mirror neurons, some people may not be ready to respond to friendly overtures. If this happens, look at it as resistance training for your brain. If you get a negative response, let it go. Don't mirror their lead. Use your PFC to sense that something must be hard for them (empathy is a core strength of the PFC, and the more you use it, the more resilient you get). Maybe wish them, sincerely, an especially good day, even if you only wish it from afar. Who knows? You may be helping them. You'll definitely be helping yourself. But one thing is clear. Turning to our tech is doing more than turning us away from more satisfying connections. It's wiring our brains to expect more predictable, linear, cause-and-effect transactions than real life in all its nonlinear joy. This can leave us feeling impatient and intolerant when we interact with others and interact authentically, which in turn fuels the cycles of loneliness. If we want change, we need to master ourselves. That starts with mastering the things that keep us from connecting, whether they're our all-too-available distractions or default habits that separate us from each other. There's an easy way to turn the tide. It starts when we unplug.

Way back in 1938, when a group of researchers asked "What makes for a good life?" they didn't know what they would learn. But they were willing to wait a long time for an answer. After watching 724 people for more than seventy-five years, they found one—something we all can learn from. The lives and fates of these 724 people, all Harvard graduates, were as individual as they were. Some lived in urban settings, some in rural. Their professions, financial success, activities, and health varied widely. Some weathered failure and loss. Some battled medical challenges. Some succeeded in their careers; some did not. One (John F. Kennedy) became a president. And some became happier than others. Across the many interviews and checkpoints that tracked these lives, those that found the most happiness credited one simple thing. Connection. Those who looked back on their lives with the greatest satisfaction were those who felt most connected to people they loved. "People who are more socially connected to family, friends, or community are happier, physically healthier, and longer-lived than others," the study revealed. "People who are more isolated than they want to be find they are less happy. Health and brain functioning decline sooner. They live shorter lives than people who feel connected." If the pull of distractions and devices is disconnecting us from family or social circles, or even making it only a little bit easier to withdraw from checking in with a friend or greeting a neighbor, are we fueling scenarios that reduce our happiness? In fairness, the Harvard study emphasized the impact of deep, close relationships, not things like simple hellos or greetings to people we barely know.

But even casual exchanges spark healthy activity in our brains. Kindness or helpful acts may seem like things we do for others— but they also help us. Opening a door for a stranger or picking up a dropped glove—even smiling in the coffee line—can activate the chemical responses that leave us feeling uplifted and balanced. Better yet is when we share our attention with people close to us or engage in real conversation with others in our social circles. Even small steps toward truly seeing those around us can boost healthier brain activity, and (since what fires, wires) make it easier for us to take more little steps, and then bigger ones, that build our sense of connection. Think of one person in your world you've been meaning to connect with: to get to know better or to actually make time for. Surprise them: write them a note, find time to talk, or tell them about something that made you think of them. Ask them about something they enjoy, and find out why they like it. Tell them something nice you remember about them. Better yet, find something to do together that you'll both remember. You'll not only be building your bond. You'll be improving your brain—and theirs too—while creating moments that add to the scenery on your lifelong path to happiness.

Unplugging

We use our gadgets for distraction and entertainment. We use them to avoid work while giving the impression that we're actually working hard.

D ata confirms what we have all noticed: all this tech we're using isn't delivering the ease and happiness it's advertised to promise. According to a global World Economic Forum study: Digital media users often spend more hours online than they sleep, yet only 50 percent believe it improves quality of life. Five out of six tech users said they weren't sure digital consumption had a positive effect on their lives. Participants' social media use alone consumed an average of 1.8 hours (30 percent of total daily online time) per day. That same study confirmed that social skills and empathy shifted downward as people spent more time online. Stress, vulnerability to addictive behavior, and a decline in physical activity also correlated to increases in screen time.

Facts from Digital Detox, a community dedicated to helping people use tech more mindfully, drive the point home: The average American dedicates 30 percent of leisure time to the Web. Highly active Internet users are 2.5 times more likely to report depression than average users. 33 percent of people admit to hiding from family and friends to check social media. 95 percent of people use some type of electronics in the hour leading up to bed. Unplugging from tech for just one day can give some people mental and physical withdrawal symptoms.Rising Challenges Psychological disorders that didn't even exist a few years ago— Internet addiction and video gaming disorder, to name two—are now medically diagnosable. Dedicated residential treatment centers have popped up to help people recover from these dependencies. A growing community called Tech Addiction Anonymous offers twelve-step support to help people break free and stay clean. And while research indicates that excessive use of digital media can negatively influence cognitive functions, behavioral development, and even mental and physical health, we keep plugging in. We see the signs everywhere. Distracted walking accidents injure more than ten thousand people each year. In a Swedish study, heavy tech use among young adults was correlated to less sleep, more stress, and a decline in mental health. Researchers in London found that interruptions from phone calls, texts, and email at work lowered IQs as significantly as a marijuana high or a night *without sleep. Yet multiple studies confirm a consistent truth: that the average American spends more than half of his or her waking life staring at a screen. Tech is changing our lives powerfully, fast, and in ways we didn't anticipate. And anything changing our lives is also changing our brains. In the language of tech itself, we're being hacked. This increasing reliance isn't adding to our happiness. In fact, as the World Economic Forum study showed, it may be interfering with it. Our emphasis on efficiency, largely ushered in by tech, often puts us in the smile-free zone, multitasking one thing off of our list so we can get on to the next.*

It's ironic that tech's promise of more productivity, and even more connection, once meant more time for the people and things we love. In reality, our easy, always-on connectedness can pull us away from real productivity and certainly from people and things that matter. Many of us are left feeling we have less time, and we need every moment simply to keep up. Now, to be fair, there's a counterpoint to any opinion or research. For every study on how tech is limiting our happiness, another shows the opposite. Examples abound of people who've found long-lost friends, built supportive communities, and faced major hardships with the help of tech. And logically, we know tech helps us in countless ways. It can keep us connected to faraway loved ones in ways no letter or phone call could. And it can tie us to communities of support and affinity when we face hardship or build change. And it can certainly help us create, design, and share work that matters deeply to us. There are plenty of benefits to be found in tech. But every choice comes with a trade-off, as many of us feel inside.

Attention Deficits If we'd known the price we'd pay for that first seductive swipe of our finger across a glassy screen, we might have done a few things differently. In an alternate reality with full understanding, we might have taken a more measured, intentional approach to the way we let tech into our lives—and we might be feeling more calm, purposeful, connected, and in control than we do today. "Most people," asserts author and teacher Darius Foroux, "don't use technology but are rather used by it. "Apps, games, videos, articles, commercials, TV shows, are all designed to keep your attention," he continues. "So without you knowing it, you waste countless hours every week. Your attention is all over the place, but not at the right place."

To be everywhere is to be nowhere.

The brain's incredible plasticity—its ability to wire what it fires—lets it adapt to the changes we put it through in near real time, updating its maps to our reality and converting new actions to routine, unseen defaults. But the amount of time we spend on tech, and the way it interacts with our brains' cognitive and reward systems, are a far cry from what our brains evolved for. Biologically speaking, our brains didn't see this one coming. Somewhere inside, something feels off. "I didn't think it would be this way," a quiet voice might seem to say. Maybe you have felt your tech was in charge of you rather than you in charge of it. Maybe you've ended a day wondering what you actually did with your day. Maybe you've let a guilty pleasure take over and then faced the struggle of catching up with the "real" stuff the morning after. Maybe you, like so many of us, have walked away from time with a friend and realized neither of you were really present, actually paying attention, as you spoke.

Maybe you've even felt that way with a loved one at home. You're not alone. We're all feeling it. And unfortunately, it's not getting better. Changing the Path Distractions have always been part of human life. In fact, distractibility can help us. In our early human days, our response to distraction might have made our day or saved our life. Looking away from the task at hand let us spot opportunities, perhaps catching the sparkle of a rare stone on the path ahead. Maybe it helped us enjoy, even share, special moments, as when a colorful bird flitted close by. It certainly saved us from danger when a rustle in the grass put us on high alert, fight-or-flight response ready. Distractibility is part of life, helpful for survival, and one of the ways we have fun. A little break can soothe the brain, refresh us, and bring serendipity as things happen around us.

But we seem to be dealing with too much of a good thing. And nothing in our human history has prepared us—or our brains—for the carefully designed "lure 'em in!" hooks built into the tech we choose and use. Getting Hacked Always-on distractions and interruptions are changing our brains, and not in ways that build mastery and satisfaction. And as Darius Foroux suggests, it's happening by design. Books and workshops coach user experience designers to understand the brain—the better to guide the trigger-and-reward responses behind conversation, sharing, likes, loves, retweets, reloads, upgrades, and

OMGs. These are the rewards they're after, and they have the science to get what they want. Our brains, in a way, have been blindsided by their skill. What starts as a fun diversion can shift as the brain reacts and rewires to dopamine hooks...and then to the next one, leaving us craving "more, more, more!" Distraction is no path to satisfaction or mastery. Too much of anything good—be it chocolate or our favorite movie or a diet of pleasurable moments—gets less good pretty fast. "It's sucking away our quality of life," claims author and NYU professor Jonathan Safran Foer. "The more distracted we become, and the more emphasis we place on speed at the expense of depth... the less likely and able we are to care... I've found myself checking email while giving my kids a bath, jumping to the Internet when a sentence or idea doesn't come effortlessly in my writing, searching for shade on a beautiful day so I can see the screen of my phone. "Sometimes we look to tech for the easy answers—which may not really be what we want. We've gotten used to on-demand information. But are we sure those easy answers deliver happiness? "We consumers forget," he continues, "that technology always...produces certain affects... But successful companies do not. They remember and profit enormously. We forget at the expense of who we are." Our easy, endless access keeps us clicking and liking or watching "just one more" episode. Like a tequila shot, the fleeting pleasure these actions deliver may not give us anything we actually want. What seems like a good idea at the time doesn't necessarily translate into real happiness. Hacking Back Distraction, especially as delivered through tech's precisely engineered experiences, can hack the way our brains work. But by understanding and working with our brains, we have ways to hack back. It takes effort and intention: the work of the Watcher. It doesn't mean abandoning tech or winding back the clock to simpler times. We wouldn't do that even if we could. Yet by understanding the most powerful device in the world, that three-pound marvel we carry with us everywhere, we can decide—even direct—what we really want. If quick-fix enjoyment isn't giving you what you're after, if you're craving a sense of mastery in the way you work, or if a call to a deeper purpose draws you, congratulations. You're ready to unplug, at least some of the time. You can start practicing ways to lean and wean away from outside lures and automatic responses.Focus and mastery are what you'll earn in return. You may gain more sense of purpose. You may come to love the peace of quiet downtime, uninterrupted, on your own terms. You may find new enjoyments, new connections, or new practices that bring you real satisfaction. Or you may *simply come back to where you are now, but with more mindfulness and clarity. Getting back in charge is a big change for many of us. To achieve it, we may need a boost. Good news: that boost is waiting for you in the next pages as you learn to master your mind.*

Mastering Your Mind

"Be careful what you water your dreams with. Water them with worry and fear and you will produce weeds that choke the life from your dream. Water them with optimism and solutions and you will cultivate success. Always be on the lookout for ways to turn a problem into an opportunity for success. Always be on the lookout for ways to nurture your dream." —LAO TZU, CHINESE SAGE, PHILOSOPHER Mastering Your Mind 67 Mastering your mind is about focus. It's about clearing away the noise and working with your brain to move through challenges and resistance. Focused work, compared to distraction? Well, it's like the difference between a deep-tissue massage and a pat on the back. Both have their place. But no number of pats can ever create that "Aaaaah" we feel when firm pressure meets tight muscle and melts the tension away. Yet deep work takes work. We resist it, and a brain accustomed to distraction struggles with it even more. That brain messes with our minds. We tend to see successful people as lucky, or gifted, or simply born in the right place at the right time. Sure, external factors influence every fate. The right environments, teachers, or opportunities certainly favor some people to succeed. But more often it's about practice: focus, diligence, and commitment. Growth. Resilience. And overcoming the all-too-available distractions that trick us away from our goals. "Luck?" answered tennis star Serena Williams when asked about her unrivaled career. "Luck has nothing to do with it, because I have spent many, many hours, countless hours, on the court working for my one moment in time, not knowing when it would come." There's real truth in her statement. If happiness is about satisfaction, how do we know when—or how—we'll reach the goals we're working on? What if we don't? What if someone beats us to it, or the rules change right before we win the game? Maybe it's not worth trying, our unconscious or subconscious self might tell us. It didn't work before. Why would it work now?

There's a reason we pay attention. Time and focus are our most precious currency. —UNKNOWN

That invisible or default mode is right: we don't always know how hard work will pay off. We question whether the long-term rewards will be worth the short-term trade-offs. Maybe that's why we're so ready to give our attention away when a distraction comes along. Yet you probably already know—even feel, in some hardto-explain way—that no number of small, shallow tasks can deliver the satisfaction we get when we accomplish things that matter. Saying "email" or "nothing" when someone asks "What did you do today?" doesn't satisfy us or our brain's hunger for meaningful work. Yet email, or a long list of distractions that add up to nothing, can fill our time, masquerading as (or even becoming) our daily work. We want more: something deeper, something that feels uniquely ours, something with purpose. Something that leads to satisfaction and mastery, to deeper forms of happiness. The good news is we can find it. We may need to learn some new practices and leave some old ones behind. Like anything worthy, it takes work. From our curious childhoods to the night-before-finals crams of our school days to the "Where are those keys?" panics of our adult lives, our brains process information in ever-changing ways. Some ways work better than others. Try this: Which do you remember better? The first time you played in snow? Or the details of a key religious milestone from the 1500s you memorized in college? If you're like most people, you probably answered "snow." If you actually remembered an event (and you aren't a history buff), maybe you remembered the Diet of Worms, whose odd-but-real name describes a historic assembly of the Holy Roman Empire back in 1521. If you did remember that name, it probably wasn't the content that you recalled. It was the strange name, which likely stood out in that history class as a daydream interrupter, mapping itself to your existing mental maps of humor, oddities, and "invertebrates that squirm." And, voilà, all these years later, the Diet of Worms pops up. Perhaps not a good visual, but an illustration of how true learning occurs. Learning builds upon learning throughout our lives. And multisensory moments map themselves to a wider array of maps. This is especially true in childhood. Imagine your first experience of snow. The surprising crunch of a freezing white substance, the sight of little flakes floating down from the sky, the soft tickle of cold on our cheeks, maybe even the challenge of waddling in a hand-me-down parka and too-big boots: new experiences etch vivid images in our young brains. They also form a foundation for future memories that will map upon them.

Memory champions use multisensory associations to bolster their maps. When scientists scanned the brains of professional memorizers (really, such a thing exists) while they were ingraining new information, they saw something different than what they saw in ordinary folks. "Memory champions lit up different parts of their brains," explains Joshua Foer, a memory expert. "They used, or seemed to use, parts of the brain involved in spatial memory and navigation." Foer uses the timeless "Memory Palace" technique to master his retention. He actively associates visual images, bawdy humor, current events, and movement to rapidly connect new thoughts to as many existing maps as possible. He "recruits," so to speak, from sensory and experiential processing centers to anchor the thoughts he seeks to memorize. We can use this thinking to improve our own retention. If we want to ingrain information, habits, attitudes, or anything new, we can work with our brains to help them absorb and encode more efficiently. Here's how. 1 LABEL: Name what you want your brain to do. "Let's learn this new habit," or "Tonight, we'll master three conjugations." This primes your brain's attention and directs it toward a task. It also prepares it to connect with existing knowledge or action maps. Labels warm your brain up and prepare it to fire, so it's ready to wire. 2 ENCOURAGE: Imagine a positive result your new habit or knowledge will lead to, then talk about it in positive terms.

Visualize it: top athletes do this as they train to reach audacious goals. Coach yourself toward that goal the way you would a close friend. And give yourself credit as you get a bit closer to it every day. Want to take this to the next level? Invite the Watcher to join in. Having that higher self reinforce the encouragement increases your brain's sense of the experience. It may even add to maps in your PFC if you associate your progress with higher-order, mindful goals you're working on. 3 ASSOCIATE: Build mental bridges between new information or activity and maps your brain has already established. If it's a new habit, do what Stanford behavioral researcher B. J. Fogg recommends: start small, and bridge the new thing to something you already do. Want to get more organized? Jot down daily priorities after you press "brew" on your coffee maker. Want to break the unending tech habit? Shut down your laptop before you floss at night. Once your new tiny habits are established, you can add to them, building new maps step-by-step until you have a whole new habit. If it's new knowledge you're after, take a page from Foer's memory book. Associate the thought with visual images or recruit from other brain centers. Moving while visualizing, coming up with rhymes (we can all still sing the alphabet song, right?), or identifying related memories and intentionally connecting the dots: each of these strengthens the maps between established knowledge and new learning.

*4 REPEAT: Repetition speeds learning. In fact, it can even convince our brains to replace known facts with known falsehoods (the "illusory fact effect"). If you want to learn faster, extend repetition across different modes. Take what you want to learn, and write it down. Narrate it to a friend, to yourself, even to your dog. Sing about it. Put a reminder in a place you visit every day. If you slip or skip, don't worry. Start again, and your brain will bridge back to the maps you've started and continue building. Stick with it. Repetition is the glue. 5 NIGHTTIME: Your brain prunes while you're sleeping. It preserves information you're actively using and tends to let go—slowly but surely—of the stuff you're not. If you want to retain something, make sure it doesn't get pruned at night. Bring it to mind as part of your evening routine. Visualize it as you prepare for sleep. If other thoughts come up, replace them with the things you want to remember. Try using your final moments of wakefulness to remember three things: your main goal for the next day, a longer-term plan you're working on, and what you appreciated most about your day. These thoughts can override the usual nighttime brain chatter. They bring a sense of peace and purpose. And they may be waiting for you the next morning, priming you to focus on what matters and anticipate what you'll appreciate most in the day ahead. Learning is one of those brain activities that sparks a range of happy chemicals. But it can also cause stress. Remember to be patient with yourself as you convert "new" into "familiar and easy." Stress chemicals like cortisol can limit activity in certain brain areas, reducing the use of multisensory maps. So be a friend to yourself, like a helpful coach. Invite the Watcher in to join the pep talk. With time and commitment, not only will you have mastered what you wanted to learn, you'll also have built a new map for how to L*E*A*R*N* the next thing. Focus We humans are problem solvers. We (and our brains) evolved by using our intelligence to survive in the world around us. We learned to follow tracks and weave grass into useful baskets. We perfected healing remedies and gained year-over-year knowledge from the seasons and stars. Focus and diligent work shaped our early brains. It took time, care, and practiced technique to make a perfect arrowhead or to know which leaves cured a headache (or made things worse). Of course, there was always the capacity for distraction: we needed that too. Our survival depended on noticing a rustle in the grass. Our social order blossomed as we made time for rituals or laughed when the village goof-off cartwheeled* across our path. We weren't optimized, though, for a barrage of small, light activities or for hopping between different modes like a frog jumping across a pond. Happiness—the kind we want—isn't "hoppiness." It comes from satisfaction, and for that, we have to work. We probably wouldn't have survived if our ancestors had faced the onslaught of distractions we face today. Want proof? If modern pedestrians don't notice a giant Wookiee waving at them as they text their way down the street, it's a good guess our ancient predecessors, if they'd been clicking and tapping away, wouldn't have noticed a saber-toothed tiger. The rest, as they say, would have been history. Deep Work Studying, completing big projects, staying patient with long- term goals, even going out and weeding the garden: we "want" to do them, "wish" we could do them, or feel like we "should" do them. But we find easy ways to blow them off. Do we feel happy afterward? No. We may have enjoyed a guilty pleasure, but the memory of what we should have done nags at us. And reality is still waiting when the party's over. GET REAL ABOUT THE TRADE- OFFS Think about why you're doing the things that distract you and soak up your time. How do they serve you? How do the results justify the price you paid?"We are only beginning to get our minds around the costs" of constant distraction, says publishing heavyweight Andrew Sullivan, "if we are even prepared to accept that there are costs." In his article "I Used to Be a Human Being," he warns, "An endless bombardment of news, gossip, and images has rendered us manic information addicts. It broke me. It might break you, too." Knowing why you're doing something is a big step toward deciding what you want to do and how. Once you realize how routine habits or thoughts are interfering with the things you really want to master, you can start mapping your path away from the old and toward the new. HARNESS YOUR REWARD SYSTEM If dopamine motivates us to pursue goals and serotonin rewards us for achieving them, why not fire both of them up? Visualizing the path to (and results of) deep work might help. After all, it does for athletes. Early in their training, they're coached (and self-coached) to see themselves as champions. In their mind's eye, they envision the practices as well as the various challenges and victories that lead to success. As they approach the starting block, they use their mind to foresee each step ahead. You can do this too. As you prepare for deep work, break your steps down. Visualize them. What will that résumé showcase when it's ready for review? What will the garage look like when it's finally empty? Visualizing primes our brains to fire up reward chemicals, making the lure of lesser rewards (like the

DECIDE WHAT YOU CARE ABOUT Perhaps nobody gets excited about cleaning the garage. But associate the task with something that does excite you—making room for your family's bicycles, having a place to paint, or finding Aunt Thelma's long-lost butterfly collection—and your purpose becomes clear. So it goes with deep work. Remembering how your project will help your team meet its goals or how your hard work helps you live in a place you love shifts the way you relate to your work. Resistance, maybe even resentment, softens. You see the bigger picture and why the work matters. This makes you more resilient when distractions pop up. WELCOME THE "IT'S NOT EASY." You're reading this because you want more happiness, right? Because the way things are doesn't feel like the way you want them to be? But admit it...you've had some moments where you've thought, "I'll never break that habit" or "When will I find time for that?"Ah, resistance. It feels like one of the brain's strongest tendencies. Getting out of automatic routines does seem to take some work. The first step to a better way is to get excited about the challenge. If you were training for a marathon or looking to perfect your curveball, you'd know you had some heavy lifting ahead. It's the same when you're training your brain. Get as excited about that as you would about approaching that finish line or seeing the batter swing and miss. You're going to get stronger! More productive! Build mental strength! Map paths that make future changes easier! See challenge as opportunity: a way to win the lasting satisfaction of getting good at something new. That thought alone can weaken the tug of the usual distractions. PREP Sitting down for a deep work session? Plot your course. Outline. Schedule breaks. Set up your work area as if you were planning a ritual. You may not have to do these things forever, but as you're weaning away from distractions and deepening your work, preparation is low-hanging fruit. Every navigator knows that preparedness is the key to success. Polar explorer Ernest Shackleton, whose life was largely marked by restlessness and failure, ultimately found his greatest victory through preparation. When ice froze around his Antarctica-bound ship, taking it eight hundred miles off course and crushing it after ten months of helpless drifting, his foresight paid off. His organizational skills and near-obsessive planning ensured his crew of twenty-eight sailors all survived the grueling endeavor. Anything else and they would never have made it home.RECLAIM THE UPPER HAND Once again, the things *that distract us were often designed to distract us. Apps, casinos, video games, ads, political campaigns, TV serials: the people who create them are experts at using "hooks" to activate dopamine-fueled craving in your brain. They know how to keep us hanging, to get us to click just one more time. They often use science to lure us in. Well, we can use our own science to resist! Start by shifting your thoughts. Stop blaming or criticizing yourself. Move from "I'm so distractible" to "This app was engineered to distract me and make me want to keep coming back." That's different from blaming the tech (or the casino, the TV show, or whatever it is that feels like it's taking charge of you). Seeing yourself as a victim won't help you kick the habit. Understanding you're being hacked, though? That helps you look more objectively at what's happening around you. That awareness gives you options. You can summon the steps listed above to start deepening your focus on something that motivates you even more than what that ad, game, or channel tries to insist you want. They may be good...but you're better. FOCUS ON PROCESS Taking things step-by-step is the only way anything ever happens. Back in 1983, when Steve Jobs was passionately focused on creating the first Mac, he sent everyone on his team a printed page with a clear message to keep at their desks: How is the decision you're making right now helping us to ship the greatest personal computer the world has ever known on January 24, 1984?*

That message directed his team to make each step matter. Micro-decisions and small, steady prioritizations shape the path to success. Each moment will offer us trade-offs: power through or look away? Do the right thing or the easy one? Most of us already know how we feel when we choose the second option. The journey is the reward. —STEVE JOBS journey reward STICK WITH IT Distraction has been training us for a long time. Learning new ways takes work, so the first steps toward change can feel fruitless or frustrating. Keep practicing. Resistance is part of the process. See it for what it is: not a dead end, but a roadblock you can get around. Keep pushing, and remind yourself, "It's normal for this to feel hard," or "It sure feels different without those easy distractions—but I'm working toward a deeper reward." About Multitasking Sorry, but multitasking is a hoax. If you think you're good at managing a lot of details concurrently, you're probably actually good at one of these things:

TASK SWITCHING You may be extra efficient at shifting smoothly between different brain modalities. If so, congratulations. But don't trick yourself. Moving between activities taxes the brain, causing fatigue, confusion, and agitation—hardly paths to happiness. It may seem to only take a moment to check email or peek in on your "likes," but you pay the cost in time and attention as your brain works its way back to what you were doing before. INTERWEAVING We can frame several seemingly disconnected things into a bigger picture, seeing them as a whole. If calling the doctor, warming a bottle, finding your keys, and getting ready to head out into the rainstorm are all part of "find out what's wrong with the baby," your brain can organize these things into a unified task. But it's expensive, in brain terms. Orchestration like this happens in the PFC, that glucose- and oxygen-hungry area. It only works well for short periods of time. We can prolong its use in critical situations, but we'll be depleted (literally brain drained) afterward. In this case, the worried parent should be extra careful while driving, because a tired PFC doesn't integrate complex information well. And they shouldn't be surprised by exhaustion, cravings, or fragile emotions when they finally get the little one back home. Executing complex tasks, especially under stress, is draining work. We can, however, multitask when we're doing multiple routine activities. That's how we walk and chew gum at the same time. We can also balance routine physical activities with certain mental work. Though this is not without cost, as the rise of accidents related to distracted driving (and even walking!) shows. Researchers at Harvard learned that drivers who multitasked while driving were as likely to tailgate, veer, or brake too late as drivers under the influence of alcohol. Talking on the phone, it turns out, is as dangerous as drunk driving. Be aware of this brain reality. How can you use your new knowledge to increase not only focus, but safety? Everyday Mindfulness Welcome that om moment and fully tune in to your inner calm. Breaking the noise habit is one of the best ways to train our brains to focus. Stillness and quiet can also shine light on a deeper sense of what matters to us: our purpose, our priorities, and the things that bring us joy. Meditation isn't about getting rid of thoughts. It's about mastering how we respond to them: learning not to chase them or let them chase us, which we often do in default mode. It's about bringing our mind, our Watcher, our awareness—call it what you will— to our thoughts and actions. This practice can take many forms. In fact, the reason people meditate is to learn to bring mindful practices "off the cushion" and into everyday life. Breath. In. The fact *that meditation often involves intentional breath is yet another example of ancient wisdom pointing to brain-aware behavior. Mindful breathing, it turns out, changes our brains. As Christina Zelano, a professor at Northwestern's medical school, has proved, "There's a dramatic difference in brain activity...during inhalation compared with exhalation. "When you breathe in, we discovered you are stimulating neurons in the olfactory cortex, amygdala, and hippocampus and across the limbic system," Dr. Zelano reports. "When you inhale, you are synchronizing brain oscillations across the limbic network." Her research shows that the rhythm of breath affects activity in the brain areas where emotions and memory are processed. Mindfulness is about deepening awareness, and you can practice it in any setting. When cooking or eating, focus on the fragrances or textures of the food before you. When out on a walk, connect with your brain as you shift your attention from a distant mountain to the close-up textures on the bark of a tree. Sit in quiet, or use everyday life to guide your awareness: the choice is yours. Anything you do to tune away from the noise and move toward the quieter, more meaningful signal within you guides you to more balance and happiness. Getting Unstuck Sometimes the only way to clear a roadblock is to walk around it. Doing deep work, changing our focus, and building new habits take practice. It can be hard. Sometimes, as the saying goes, we get the bear. Sometimes...well, you know the rest. If it's the warm fuzzy bear of serotonin you're after, remember that even the ancient Greeks knew satisfaction took long-term work and lots of practice. Sometimes we get stuck. We run out of steam. Or something happens that takes us jarringly off path. Or we simply need more than our current brain state seems to offer.*

Don't panic. You have choices, ones that reinforce your happiness practice and cross over to many other life scenarios. SHIFT GEARS If you're working on a computer, get out your pen and paper. Maybe walk around talking about the problem. Record that, and listen back. This will help you organize and map the information in different ways. Who knows? Maybe you and your brain will map your way to an answer. TALK NICE To yourself, that is. Avoid self-criticism. Our subconscious mind has a way of pointing the problem back at us when we hit a skid. If you try to change a habit or do everything you can to focus and it still doesn't work, give yourself a break. Reflect on why you're stuck and what skills you can call on to move forward. What can you do? Encourage yourself as you would a treasured friend. You may see your next steps in a whole new light. REPLENISH Take a moment to make sure you're taking extra good care of your body. Your roadblock may simply be a tired PFC, depleted by hunger, fatigue, stress, or other brain drains. Get up. Stretch. Get a glass of water or something nourishing to eat. Meditate, even for ten minutes. Remember, your brain and your body are part of one system. Caring for one creates good for the other. OPTIMIZE FOR AHA "Aha moments" happen by surprise, as the name suggests, when two or more previously unconnected ideas find each other through a new connection and, whoosh, a new brain pathway is formed. You can almost feel it—but you can't force it. To increase the likeliness of an aha moment, shift gears. Seek sensory input that's different from what you've been trying. There's a reason so many people get their best ideas in the shower: the sound and feel of water, the warmth, calm, or maybe even the ions shift something in the brain and open it to insight. You have to collect the right dots before you can connect them. Go find yourself a few more dots. TAKE A BREAK You can run screaming from the roadblock or see it as a workout partner. Either may work, but one (guess which?) tends to work better. Plan a hike, or even a walk around the block, and tell your brain, "Time for a clean slate," or "How about a nature break?" Whatever you do—running a load of laundry, reading, or going for a leg-pumping bike ride—do it attentively. Absorb yourself in it. Watch the details. Focus on how you're doing what you're doing. Often, we do the opposite. We take the stress of a roadblock with us and go through the motions of doing something else. Yet awakening your senses by creating a completely different experience refreshes the brain. It may replenish the idea supply in the very brain areas you need to get around that block. As we learn to take mindful, intentional charge of how we use our brains, we direct ourselves increasingly toward choices and activities that bring more satisfaction—and help strengthen our highest-level cognitive abilities. That, it turns out, fuels satisfaction in and of itself. And things get even better when we use our new mastery to activate our brains.

It would be one thing if Wim Hof hiked to the top of Czechia's highest peak in −27°F weather, wearing only shorts, all alone. Then you could call him an outlier: someone possessing a mutant layer of insulating fat, a mind of absolute steel, or a very unusual metabolism. But he didn't hike alone. In multiple summits of that peak, Hof brought companions: dozens of them, women and men, early twenties through midsixties, from all corners of the globe. They all climbed, lively and smiling, astonishing border guards and medical professionals as they gleefully reached the top and celebrated (one group danced the Harlem Shuffle), clad, basically, in beachwear. Some say it's Hof's charismatic personality. "Just being in his presence inspired us to accomplish things we never would have normally done," said one climber. But watch Hof, and you'll learn it's something more. Hof teaches his devotees an unusual breathing technique: deep breaths with partial exhales followed by prolonged holds. It's easy to learn, and the proof starts fast. After a short orientation, Hof guides his mentees into increasingly long cold-water plunges or sessions of sprawling nearly naked in snow. Almost from the get-go, his students express awe at not feeling cold. After four days, they're ready to scale an icy mountain. If this were only Hof, you'd think he was a hoax. But countless scientists have monitored his abilities, marveling at how he can stand, say, in a huge box of ice for nearly two hours while maintaining his body's core temperature. Or how he climbed to twenty-two thousand feet at Mount Everest, reached the summit of Mount Kilimanjaro in only two days; ran a full marathon above the Arctic Circle, clad only in shoes and shorts; and aced another marathon in Africa's Namib Desert (where temperatures often reach 113°F) without drinking water. Hof achieved each of these feats under rigorous medical and scientific supervision. How does he do it? And how does he teach others to join the "fun"? Turns out, Hof uses the power of his mind to take control of the invisible: the unconscious, and normally autonomous, brain regions that control the body and the central nervous system. "Breathing and intention change things," he has said. "They get us beneath fear, back to the unconditioned nature and inner power we all have. We learn to control what's within ourselves, reclaiming our true happiness, health, and strength. It's not philosophical. It's chemical. And anyone can do it." Hof may have mastered a form of mind control also cultivated by Tibetan Tummo meditators. In their practice, breath, visualization, and a shutdown of mental activity let them convert body energy into heat. Experiments on these meditators documented temperature increases of nearly 12°F in their fingers and toes and noteworthy changes to core body temperature. Hof's mastery, though, goes beyond temperature control. Under intense medical scrutiny, he has been injected with bacterial by-products that ordinarily cause extreme chills, aches, and fever. As doctors prodded and measured, Hof took control and suppressed his body's reaction. What's more, twelve trainees joined him in that adventure, also avoiding illness. There's *something to the breathing that stimulates an adrenaline response, but Hof says it's more than that. He believes we all have more control of our autonomous systems than we've been conditioned to believe. "Everyone is able to do much more than is thought of," he insists.*

"Enlightenment is a state of happiness and health, and it's not as distant as we're told it is. "We can learn to control our body from within our body. This is our natural ability. Anyone can do this. My dream is to show everyone how."

Activating

T he brain is a powerful instrument—an extraordinary powerhouse ready to help us navigate nearly any situation life might bring our way. Yet there's something even more powerful than this three-pound marvel: you. When you direct this "most complicated object in the known universe," working with your brain, you're at your best. But as you've learned, it takes new intentions, actions, and attitudes master this ability. In Charge, On Purpose What do you want more than the easy indulgences dangled out there to distract you from your path? How will you get there? What's the first step, whatever it might be, that points you in that direction?And why do you want that achievement or experience? What makes you excited, curious, or hungry to pursue it? Ask yourself these questions and listen openly to what comes up. Really...listen. Don't be surprised if a voice inside you tries toshut your excitement down. Remember, the brain tends to preserve the thoughts and actions you've already taken, resisting the effort and perceived risks often associated with new thoughts. Don't worry if that happens. It's normal. But keep asking, and stay mindful of the answers. Somewhere in them you'll find clues to what really matters to you. Something in your answers may spark embers of empathy or strike chords of passion. What you hear may help you identify something you want to make better, in the world or in your life, through intention and contribution. It might be a small thing. We live in a time where big problems overwhelm us, so we often expect ourselves to think big. It's easy to forget that small actions can spark big changes. Your answer might point you to creating a loving home or to supporting people who face obstacles. It may be as simple as creating art or telling stories that build understanding (or break down walls). Maybe it points to curing a disease, slowing climate change, or facing a political problem in a way that visibly changes the world. But it doesn't need to be. Things as small as bringing renewable bags to the grocery store, de-escalating an angry conversation, or telling your child how you admire the way they said thank you at dinner: any of those things can align us with purpose. Any of those things can help change the world. A lot of people expect their purpose to be a job title, an epic achievement, or maybe something that changes countless lives. It's easy to understand where that expectation might come from, especially in the high-pressure times we all live in. The noise around us glorifies the few who rise to power, wealth, or public acclaim.

Meanwhile, much in the world is held together by the actions of countless people whose essential contributions simply never win acclaim. That doesn't make those contributions any less important. "Purpose" doesn't have to be about some large-scale external achievement. It may be about the way you do something—kindly, or as part of a community. It may be about the way you spend time—encouraging others, or being a healthy role model. Perhaps it's about bringing more beauty to the world, through something you create, something you nurture, or simply the way you live. Or even about bringing security and confidence to those you love, which is perhaps one of the greatest purposes of all.

Maybe it is about improving something large scale: aligning with a path you deeply believe in, even if it means risking the ease and approval of a more ordinary life. Whatever it is, learning to listen to yourself, and tuning away from the easy distractions that can scramble our signals of truth, is a first step in tuning in to more What you do makes a difference, and you have to decide what kind of difference you want to make. —JANE GOODALL, WILDLIFE RESEARCHER, ANTHROPOLOGIST, U.N. MESSENGER OF PEACE

purpose and satisfaction. It's hard to break free of the noise. Yet it's a time-honored path to greater happiness. Whether your purpose is to change the world or simply to change your world, look inside, and trust what you find there. "Collect the dots" around your deepest wishes and the things that bring you the greatest satisfaction. As your collection grows, the connections, too, will become more clear. We're here to contribute, and our brains know it. And that's what this book is really about: awakening a memory in you that may have gotten lost in all of the noise and distraction of everyday life. You are here for a reason, and your reason is worthy. Your happiness stems from knowing and acting on that, even as distractions dangle around you. The journey of happiness is mapped by your brain, but it's directed by you. As you recognize invisible or default modes and shift to intentional thinking, you are already clearing your path to success. Now, the journey begins. Between you and your brain, you have all it takes to find what you're looking for.

Back in the eighties, Pamela Weiss was a recent college graduate and newly-minted professional working for a health-care consulting practice. She had a mission: improving the quality of medical care to people like herself, a Type 1 diabetic since age ten. Her illness had blocked her from lifelong dreams of travel and adventure. Yet, determined as she was to fight the condition, her job wasn't cutting it. Spreadsheets and endless reports were not what she had in mind. She was bored, frustrated, and dissatisfied. That's when Weiss discovered San Francisco Zen Center. She was taken aback by the kindness and peace of the community she met there. Whatever they've got, I want, she thought. She became so drawn in, she decided to forgo graduate school and dedicate herself to the rigor of Zen Buddhist training. That was over thirty years ago. Today, Weiss is a Buddhist teacher whose work is rooted in the psychology and discipline of Buddhist practice. "Most of us move through life wanting pleasant experiences and resisting unpleasant ones," she explains. "Largely, 'I like it' or 'I don't like it' defines our experience. "This may work temporarily. But it doesn't last. Buddhism teaches that becoming objectively present to our moment-tomoment experience allows us to shift from reacting habitually to responding appropriately." Appropriate response is a term from one of Weiss's favorite Zen teaching stories. "A student visits an honored teacher in his final hours," she shares. "He asks, 'What is the teaching of your entire lifetime?' Likely, the student expected a big, enlightening answer. But in the spare simplicity of Zen wisdom, the master simply replied, 'An appropriate response.'" The term is also the name of the leadership development practice Weiss founded, elevating principled, mindful leadership in some of Silicon Valley's best known companies. "'Appropriate response' is the essence of what so many of us seek—and seek to provide," she explains. "We all face struggles and dilemmas. Life can feel overwhelming, even though we are smart, capable people. What we need are practices and perspectives that allow us to meet the complexity with clarity, courage, and kindness." Her current work focuses on shaping a new model for leadership based on the Buddhist concept of a Bodhisattva. "Bodhisattva is a term bursting with richness and meaning," she says. "Bodhi means awake, enlightened, or wise. Sattva means sentient being. Bodhisattva leadership means having the awareness to master the perceptions and feelings of the human experience so we can be helpful to others, sharing wisdom and kindness in skillful ways." Her goal? To have the term bodhisattva shape a new narrative for leaders of all kinds. "Bodhisattvas understand our place in the web of all being," she explains. "Our health as humans is intricately tied to the health of our planet, the health of all others. Bodhisattva leadership is fueled by *the wish to increase this health and well-being, alleviating suffering and expanding freedom and joy. My vision is for the word 'bodhisattva' to define our sense of leadership within the next decade. Given the complexity and divisiveness of our time, I see this as an essential path. "Buddhist teaching and the bodhisattva path offer a framework for realizing genuine contentment," Weiss concludes. "Happiness means true satisfaction: beyond fleeting moments of pleasant experience. My aspiration is to make this understanding available as widely as I can."*

Taking Charge

Your time is limited, so don't waste it living someone else's life... Don't let the noise of others' opinions drown out your own inner voice. And most important, have the courage to follow your heart and intuition. They somehow already know what you truly want to become. —STEVE JOBS When I was in grade school, they told me to write down what I wanted to be when I grew up. I wrote down "happy." They told me I didn't understand the assignment. I told them they didn't understand life. —UNKNOWN Taking Charge 101 A s the deeply satisfying journey of writing this book was coming to a close, I stepped outside for a breath of fresh air. A neighbor was out for a walk, and we said hello. She was visibly sad. She started talking about her frustration and feelings of helplessness as she thought about the many difficult conditions in today's world. "It's all so hard," she said. "And there's nothing I can do to make a difference." One thing I've always appreciated about this neighbor is how she makes eye contact. A former professional dancer, her warm brown eyes and wavy white hair make her lovely to look at. Yet her eyes were sad as she spoke about all that troubled her. It was clear she'd been thinking about this—and her sense of helplessness—a lot. "It kills me to think there's nothing I can do," she said, a tinge of anger in her voice. As I looked at her, I wondered what my mirror neurons were doing and if that was oxytocin I felt activating my sense of empathy. I could have reacted. My automatic mode would gladly have jumped in, egging her on and perhaps escalating the despair. "I know!" I could have said. "It makes me so angry that..." inserting whatever opinion or news story seemed to add to the sense of outrage. But I slowed down and found a different response. "You are doing something," I told her. She looked curious. "Whenever I talk with you, I notice how you make eye contact. You really connect. I'll bet you do that often when you interact with people." She wavered, glancing away. After a moment, though, she looked back, nodding. "People do seem to say that from time to time."

So I gave her a mini lecture—exactly the type of thing that tends to annoy my sons—on mirror neurons. I told her how simple things like eye contact actually helped shift people from routine, automatic patterns and into more awareness. And how awareness can activate the parts of our brains that improve mood, social connection, and impulse control. Her kind eye contact, I suggested, might help others treat someone else more kindly, catalyzing a virtuous chain of "pass it on." Her gaze softened. Her expression looked more hopeful. She reached over and squeezed my hand. (Take that, sons!) "It reminds me," she said, a hint of excitement in her voice, "of that thing Gandhi said. You know: 'Be the change you want to see in the world.'" "Exactly," I agreed. She twinkled, then shrugged. "If it's good enough for Gandhi, I guess it's good enough for me." My life is my message. —MAHATMA GANDHI It's never too late to get back in charge, as my lovely neighbor illustrates. If I'd thought it was too late ten years ago, I would never have written this book. Around that time, my coworker Marlene shared a saying she'd learned from her grandmother, who had emigrated to the United States from China. It goes like this:"When you stand at the bottom of a mountain and look up, all you see are the things that block your path. Yet when you reach the top and look down, you will know: one hundred paths would have brought you to that place." Happiness, real happiness, is calling you. You can bring it to your life. And everything on your path so far, even when you least believe it, has brought you to the place where you are ready to find more of it. We think we have to be fearless to move forward, toward happiness and the deeper satisfaction we seek. Sure. Except fearless is actually two words in one, and when you take them apart, you get a new message: Fear less. That is truly all it takes: fear less. Even a little bit less. Summon your Watcher. Smile at your threat state or automatic mode, and reassure it. Tell it, "Go on break. I've got this." And then take a step. You, after all, have the most powerful object in the known universe on your side. It's watching you, this very moment, ready to learn from what you do next. Whatever you choose, it is ready to help you do more of. It's on your side. And now you know how to work with it too. It's ready, and so are you. Welcome to your first step toward more happiness—and the satisfaction you deserve.